# The Accounting Tabloid
## Receivables, Simply Explained

The Handbook of choice

Othneil Hall

abbott press

Copyright © 2017 Othneil Hall.

All rights reserved. No part of this book may be used or reproduced by any means, graphic, electronic, or mechanical, including photocopying, recording, taping or by any information storage retrieval system without the written permission of the author except in the case of brief quotations embodied in critical articles and reviews.

Abbott Press books may be ordered through booksellers or by contacting:

Abbott Press
1663 Liberty Drive
Bloomington, IN 47403
www.abbottpress.com
Phone: 1 (866) 697-5310

Because of the dynamic nature of the Internet, any web addresses or links contained in this book may have changed since publication and may no longer be valid. The views expressed in this work are solely those of the author and do not necessarily reflect the views of the publisher, and the publisher hereby disclaims any responsibility for them.

Any people depicted in stock imagery provided by Thinkstock are models, and such images are being used for illustrative purposes only. Certain stock imagery © Thinkstock.

ISBN: 978-1-4582-1432-4 (sc)
ISBN: 978-1-4582-1433-1 (hc)
ISBN: 978-1-4582-1434-8 (e)

Library of Congress Control Number: 2014902869

Print information available on the last page.

Abbott Press rev. date: 10/18/2017

# The Purpose of this Book

This book was written to assist as best as possible those individuals who are somewhat new to the field of accounting and the topic of receivables. It will help you understand how to record the journal entries relating to a diversity of transactions regarding receivables. It is kept very simple (just as 1, 2, 3). This book gives you a very broad perspective on receivables. Therefore, if you are employed or thinking of getting employed as a manager or bookkeeper in charge of receivables, office manager or accounting clerk, then here is an opportunity to be exposed to information that can be of help towards your goal.

This book will help you to handle transactions for a service oriented company as well as one that trades in merchandise inventory. There are some transactions that the journal entries are similar between the two types of businesses; however, once there is a difference with regards to the recording of any transaction, we will provide you with the dual explanation of the journal entry.

# Acknowledgements

When I decided to pen this book, there were some uncertainties as to the format or the structure to use in putting it together. Nonetheless, after ongoing dialogues with some of my colleagues, I was able to arrive at a conclusion for the formatting style.

With the achievement of this objective, I am happy to express my sincere gratitude to all those who have helped and encouraged me along the way. It is my pleasure to make special mention of Professor Joel Barker and Supplemental Instruction Supervisor Rahshemah Floyd for their assistance with the editorial work, also accounting major Karlene Marston for her daily encouragements.

The others not mentioned above, your inputs are also very much appreciated. I assure you all that I am forever grateful.

With pride and joy, this journey has been completed, and we look forward, as usual, to continue working together in producing more useful materials that can help others who are interested in understanding the language of business.

Again, thank you all.

# Contents

Some important things to remember ..... 1
Receivables ..... 11
Credit balance in accounts receivable ..... 25
Lock Box Banking ..... 26
Handling Discount ..... 27
Analysis of Accounts Receivable ..... 34
Sales Returns and Allowances ..... 39
Transportation Cost ..... 45
Valuing Accounts Receivable ..... 47
Credit Card Payments ..... 67
Sales in Foreign Currency ..... 69
Notes Receivable ..... 72
Valuation of Notes Receivable ..... 97
Disposition (Selling) of Accounts Receivable ..... 100
Pledging of receivables ..... 106
Some important Ratios ..... 108
Rent receivable ..... 110
Lease Receivable ..... 111
Interest receivable ..... 119
Dividends Receivable ..... 120
Cash advances to employees ..... 121
Income Tax Receivable ..... 123
Insurance Claims Receivable ..... 126
Sales on Installment ..... 128
Retainage ..... 130
Loans Receivable ..... 132
Factoring Arrangement ..... 133
Rebates ..... 134
Investment in Debt Securities ..... 135

Investment in Equity Securities ................................................... 137
Letter of Credit ................................................................................ 138
Standby Commitment ................................................................... 140
Mini cases ........................................................................................ 141

Glossary ........................................................................................... 145
Index ................................................................................................ 151

# Some important things to remember

- Accounting transactions are about making double entries of debits and credits.
- You must be able to analyze each transaction before journalizing them. That is determining how each transaction affects the asset, liability or equity account.
- All accounting transactions must be journalized first. Although with modern computer software, once you have entered a transaction based on a document such as an invoice via the computer, the software skillfully handles everything behind the scene.
- A journal is the book of original entry that the transactions are recorded in by order of the date the transactions occurred. Most companies have separate journals for credit sales, credit purchases, cash receipts, cash disbursements and general journal entries. If they do not have a journal for each of these tasks, they will at least have a general journal for the recording of all transactions.
- For every debit entry, there has to be a corresponding credit entry, and for every credit entry, there has to be a corresponding debit entry.
- Total debits must equal total credits.
- Accounting equation: Assets = Liabilities + Equity.
  $$\$2,200 = 650 + 1550$$

## Illustration 1

| | |
|---|---:|
| Assets are the value of things you own | $2,200 |
| Liabilities are the value of what you owe | (650) |
| Equity is simply the difference between what you own and what you owe, (which equates to your claim on the assets). | <u>1,550</u> |

What this means, is that, if the owner decides to sell the assets at this moment, he/she collects cash $2,200. Pays the liabilities of $650 and retains $1,550.

# The Accounting Cycle

The accounting cycle refers to the sequence of steps that lead up to the preparation of the financial statements. This process starts with the analysis of transactions to mostly the preparation of the post-closing trial balance. The accounting cycle is vital to understand since it is the structure upon which accounting is designed.

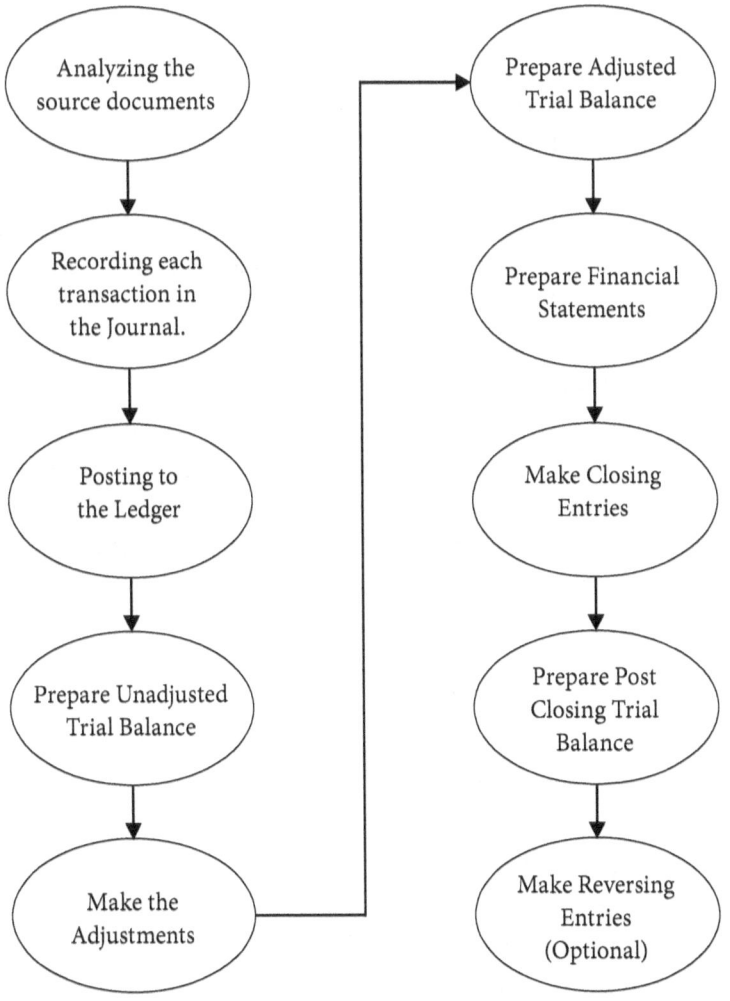

# The explanation of the Accounting Cycle

1. **Analyzing the source documents**
   This step is the first part of the process when the source documents such as invoices or checks are analyzed, to determine how they affect asset, liability or equity.

2. **Recording the transactions in the Journal**
   The transactions are then recorded in the journal. For example, if the source documents are sales invoices; these invoices are recorded as debits to accounts receivable and credits to Sales or Service Revenue.
   **Note: If your accounting system is computerized, once you have entered the invoices to the system, the software automatically does the debit and credit entries in both the journal and the ledger behind the scene.**

3. **Posting the transactions to the ledger**
   After recording the transactions in the journal, post the entries to the respective accounts in the ledger (e.g., the record keeping of the customer accounts is the accounts receivable ledger). That is, an update to the individual customer account with each amount as a debit entry, and update to the sales account with the corresponding credit entry.

4. **The preparation of the unadjusted trial balance**
   Each account balance in the ledger is used to produce the unadjusted trial balance.

5. **Make the adjustments**
   At this stage, any adjusting entries necessary are now made. There are five categories of adjusting entries:

I. Prepaid expenses- adjusting for expired or used amounts.
II. Depreciation which systematically and rationally allocates the cost of assets over a given period.
III. Accrued expenses - Expenses incurred but not yet paid.
IV. Accrued revenue - Revenue earned, but the business has not yet collected the cash.
V. Unearned revenue - Cash collected in advance, but the business has not yet earned the revenue.

**Note that, the making of an adjusting entry always affect an income statement revenue or expense account, and a balance sheet asset or liability account.**

6. **Prepare adjusted trial balance**
After making the adjusting entries to the previous ledger balances, the adjusted trial balance is then prepared according to the new balances.

7. **Prepare statements**
The adjusted trial balance is now used to prepare the financial statements.

8. **Closing Entries**
Close temporary accounts by journalizing and posting.

9. **Prepare post-closing trial balance**
A post-closing trial balance is now prepared.

10. **Reversal entries**
This step is optional.

## FOB (Free on Board) Shipping Point

The buyer is responsible for paying the shipping or transportation cost. Ownership of the merchandise inventory is passed from the seller to the buyer once the goods are loaded on an accepted means of transportation. That means, even though the goods are in transit, they are now part of the buyer's inventory and any risk associated with the goods while in transit are undertaken by the buyer.

**Note that, under FOB shipping point arrangement, there are times when the seller pays the shipping cost, and the buyer has to reimburse the seller.**

## FOB (Free on Board) Destination Point

The seller is responsible for paying the shipping or transportation cost. Ownership of the merchandise inventory is not passed to the buyer until the goods arrive at the buyer's place of business. That means the seller undertakes the risk involved in transporting the goods and cannot record a sale until the goods reach the buyer (goods are part of the seller's inventory while they are in transit).

# How Debits and Credits affect the three Main Types of Balance Sheet Accounts

| Debit | Credit |
|---|---|
| Increase in asset accounts | Decrease in asset accounts |
| Decrease in liability accounts | Increase in liability accounts |
| Decrease in equity accounts | Increase in equity accounts |

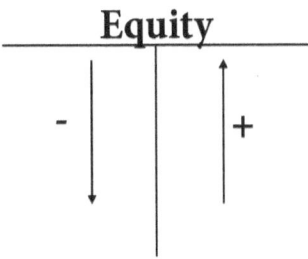

## How Debits and Credits affect the two Main Types of Income Statement Accounts

| Debit | Credit |
|---|---|
| Increase in expense accounts (Reduction to equity) | Decrease in expense accounts (Addition to equity) |
| Decrease in revenue accounts (Reduction to equity) | Increase in revenue accounts (Addition to equity) |
|  |  |

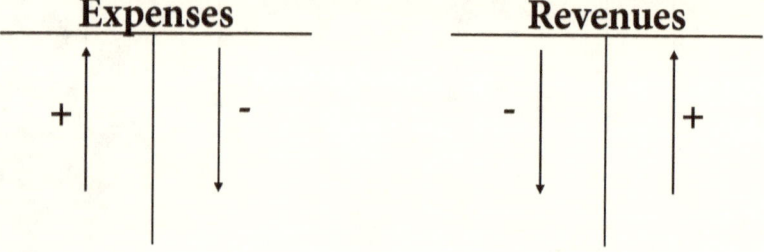

# The Normal Balances of Accounts

> Accounts have normal balances on the side where the increases are recorded

- Asset accounts have normal balances on the *debit side.*
- Expense accounts have normal balances on the *debit side.*
- Liability accounts have normal balances on the *credit side.*
- Equity accounts have normal balances on the *credit side.*
- Revenue accounts have normal balances on the *credit side.*

## Illustration 11

A Simple Income Statement Presentation

| | |
|---|---:|
| Revenue | $1,500 |
| Operating Expenses | (900) |
| Net Operating Income | 600 |

# Illustration 111

## A Simple Balance Sheet presentation

**Assets**
| | |
|---|---|
| Current assets | $1,000 |
| Non-current Assets | <u>1,200</u> |
| Total assets | <u>2,200</u> |

**Liabilities**
| | |
|---|---|
| Current liabilities | 150 |
| Long-term liabilities | 200 |

**Equity**
| | |
|---|---|
| Preferred stocks | 500 |
| Common stocks | 750 |
| Retained earnings | <u>600</u> |
| Total liabilities & equity | <u>2,200</u> |

# Receivables

Whenever a Company performs a financial transaction with individuals or other companies, and it plans to collect the cash at a future date, these impending cash collections are referred to as *receivables*.

Just for the purpose of this book, we look at a very simple definition of receivables as, *"the name given for any claims to be collected in monetary value."* Therefore, when we think of receivables, our focus should be on the money owed to a company by outsiders or even by employees that are capable of collecting. The receivables can be created by either trade or non-trade activities. If the company is using an accrual system of accounting, the trade receivables are the money the company would have recognized most times as revenue earned even though they have not collected the cash as yet.

As a result of the accrual system of accounting, these future collections (receivables) cannot go un-noticed. We must recognize these receivables on the books at the point in time they are created, and because the collection is at a future date, they are considered as economic items that provide future value to the company that plans to collect them.

The Financial Accounting Standards Board (FASB)-Codification 310 has simply referred to receivables as "that which may arise from credit sales, loans or other transactions." They may be in the form of loans, notes and other types of financial instruments and may be originated by an entity or purchased from another entity.

Under the United States Generally Accepted Accounting Principles (GAAP), the FASB Codification 310 has provided a guide as to how we should treat these receivables. The argument is simply that since these receivables have proven to have some future economic value and that they belong to the company; it is now easy to conclude that they are part of the family of assets. Since they are assets, it means that they are also a balance sheet item. The classification of these assets on the balance sheet can either be current assets or long term/non-current assets. If collections are expected to be within one year or the operating cycle, whichever is longer, the receivables are part of current assets. Otherwise, they are non-current or long-term assets.

Most companies tend to list on their balance sheet a single line item of their total receivables, with further explanation in the notes or as an appendix to the financial statements.

### Illustration 1V

The balance sheet extract below shows Ford Motor Company presentation of total net receivables (Gross receivables less allowance for doubtful accounts) on their balance sheet. (*Source:* Yahoo Finance)

# Balance Sheet Extract of Ford Motor Company

| Period Ending | Dec 30, 2012 | Dec 30, 2011 | Dec 30, 2010 |
|---|---|---|---|
| **Assets** | | | |
| **Current Assets** | | | |
| Cash and Cash Equivalents | 15,659,000 | 17,148,000 | 14,805,000 |
| Short Term Investments | 20,284,000 | 18,618,000 | 20,765,000 |
| **Net Receivables** | **82,338,000** | **78,541,000** | **8,381,000** |
| Inventory | 7,362,000 | 5,901,000 | 5,917,000 |
| Other Current Assets | - | - | - |
| **Total Current Assets** | **125,643,000** | **120,208,000** | **49,868,000** |
| **Non-Current Assets** | | | |
| Long Term Investments | 3,246,000 | 2,936,000 | 72,639,000 |
| Property Plant and Equipment | 41,393,000 | 35,209,000 | 34,854,000 |
| Goodwill | - | - | - |
| Intangible Assets | 87,000 | 100,000 | 102,000 |
| Accumulated Amortization | - | - | - |
| Other Assets | 5,000,000 | 4,770,000 | 5,221,000 |
| Deferred Long Term Asset Charges | 15,185,000 | 15,125,000 | 2,003,000 |
| **Total Assets** | **190,554,000** | **178,348,000** | **164,687,000** |

## Some examples of receivables and their sources

While the following list does not include all the possible descriptions and sources of receivables, we have provided you with a list of the most popular ones to date.

**Accounts receivable or trade receivable**
**Sales in foreign currency**
**Notes receivable**
**Rent receivable**
**Lease receivable**
**Interest and dividends receivable**
**Cash advances to employees**
**Tax refund receivable**
**Insurance claims receivable**
**Sales on installment**
**Retainage**
**Loans receivable**
**Factoring arrangement**
**Rebates**
**Debt security**
**Letter of credit**
**Standby commitment to purchase loans**

We will examine each of the above regarding the recording entries.

## Accounts Receivable/Trade Receivables

This is the money owed to a particular company by customers for goods sold or services provided to them on credit. These customers promise to pay, for example within a 30-60 days' time frame, and since these payments are expected to be received by the company within one year, they are classified and reported as part of current assets on the balance sheet.

Even though "cash is king" and every company is aware of such, our major concern might be why do companies continue to sell on credit.

The selling of any goods or the provision of any services only on a cash basis may not help most businesses. Therefore, companies take the risk of extending credit to their customers in an attempt to increase their sales.

While the intention behind the idea is a good one, some challenges are involved with the issuing of credit. Nonetheless, having a management team that can implement an effective credit policy, some of these problems can be mitigated or minimized.

## An Effective Accounts Receivable System

Remember that a poor cash flow can be disastrous for any business entity. Therefore, before a company gives credit to any new customer, credit checks of the customer are required so as to minimize any risk involved in the process. Companies that sell on credit need to have as best as possible, an effective and efficient accounts receivable system in place so as to facilitate the smooth collection of the cash from the hands of the customers.

Management should ensure that each section of their accounts receivable department runs as efficiently as possible so that it produces the desired result.

There are some things that a company can do to help their system of collection:

- **The numbering of invoices:** Invoices must have a numbering sequence for effective control.
- **Dispatching of invoices:** Companies must ensure that invoices are dispatched as early as possible so as to let the customers be aware of the seriousness about cash collection. If customers see that you have little or no care in sending out your invoices early, they too in return may display a lack of urgency in paying any money owed.
- **The accuracy of invoices:** There is an absolute need for the correctness of any invoice sent to a customer. The invoice must state accurately the amount owed, the due date for payment, discount allowed if any, the description of the items sold and any other pertinent information that needs to be conveyed. Owing customers most times take advantage of errors on the invoices by delaying payment of the invoices until they are contacted. The time required to effect the necessary correction is time lost in collecting and utilizing your cash.
- **Credit card payment:** Some companies implement a system of having their customers' credit card details on hand so that they can easily charge the amount due on the invoices against their accounts. While this type of arrangement is good, effective internal controls are needed so as to prevent mistakes and fraud.
- **Store card:** Some retail stores issue store cards to their customers, in this case, the amount owed by the customers

at most times starts attracting interest from the date of the purchase. This type of arrangement can be a huge advantage for the retail stores because it allows them to escape the fees charged by credit card companies. Monthly statements are then sent out to these customers who have the option of making at least a minimum payment.

- **Accounts receivable reconciliation:** Whenever goods or services are sold or provided on credit to customers, it is advisable to try our utmost to keep an accurate record of all the accounts receivable and invoices outstanding. In order to have proper checks and balances, it is good for the company to keep a second set of records in Microsoft Excel as a support for the information in the journal and ledger. The comparison can be made to detect any discrepancy.
- **Employee training:** Companies must also ensure that their employees receive the necessary training to do the job. Not having adequately trained employees can result in the loss of money to companies. The employees must be taught the following:
  - how to handle the collection of payments,
  - how to make adjustments as it relates to disputes and write-offs concerning the customers' accounts,
  - how to conduct follow-ups to ensure that the customers are satisfied,
  - how to push aggressively for the collection of any cash outstanding without pushing the customer away since client retention is also an objective.

- **Collection agency:** There is a need to have an excellent collection agency in place should there be a need for one. They are required specifically to help in the collection of

overdue accounts so as to avoid excessive writing off of bad debts.
- **Periodic Audit:** Management needs to have periodic audit of the accounts receivable system to ensure compliance. Therefore, the system and procedure need to be adequately documented.
- **Open door policy:** Having an open door policy so that staff members can feel free to communicate ideas or any other relevant inputs so as to improve the system.

# A Typical Accounts Receivable System

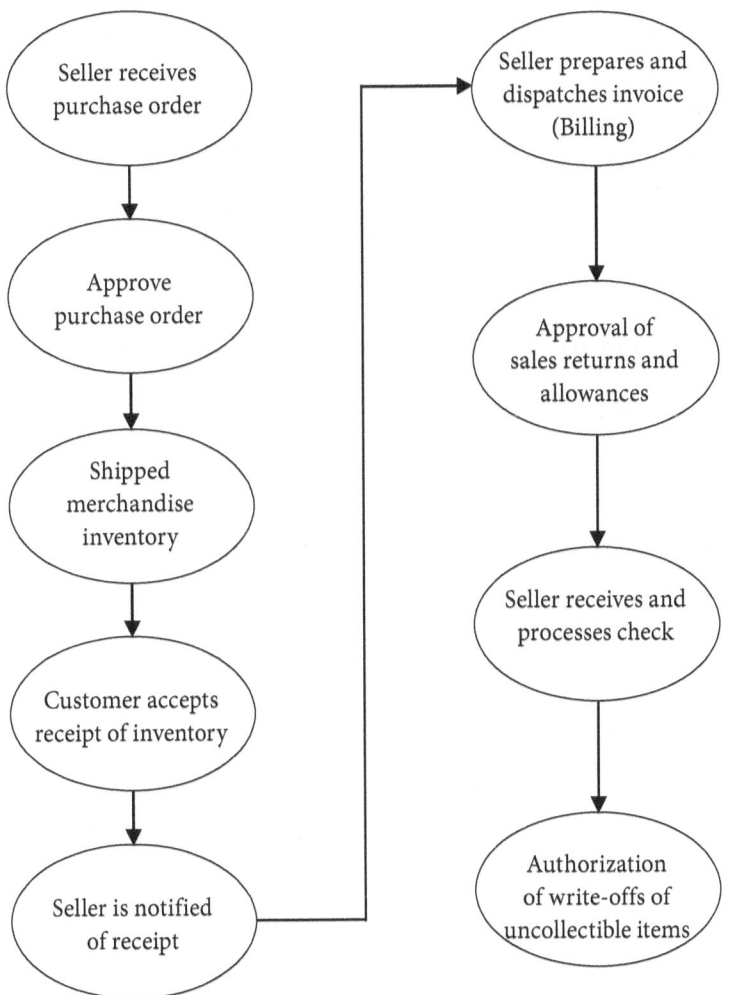

It is always good to have separation of duties within any accounts receivable system as part of effective internal controls over credit sales.

## Recognizing your accounts receivable

As a general practice in the real business world, an account receivable is recognized when the invoice is sent out to the customer. Therefore, whenever a credit sale is made, that is the goods have been delivered (title passed), or the service has been rendered, you should ensure that the invoice is prepared and dispatched immediately to the customer.

The company making the sale records the amount in the journal as a **debit to accounts receivable and a credit to sales or service revenue.**

There are two sample companies used in our examples; they are Premier Business Services NY: A Company that mostly offers Accounting, Tax Preparation, Payroll and QuickBooks Consultancy Services and JOAH Trading: A Company that sells merchandise inventory.

# Illustration V

## Sample of an invoice

---

**JOAH Trading**                                **INVOICE: 001**

Street Address, City, State                     Date
Phone: 888-888-8888 | Fax: 555-555-5555
www.joahaddress.com

**TO:**
Company X
Street Address, City, State
Phone: 999-999-9999 | Fax: 666-666-6666
www.comaddress.com

| Sales Rep. | P.O. Number | Ship Date | Ship Via | FOB | Terms |
|---|---|---|---|---|---|
|  |  |  |  |  |  |

| Quantity | Description | Unit Price | Total |
|---|---|---|---|
|  |  |  |  |

**Make all checks payable to JOAH Trading**

**THANK YOU FOR YOUR BUSINESS!**

## Illustration V1

On January 1, 2015, Premier Business Services provided tax accounting services to company Y and company Z for $980 and $1,020 respectively on credit and collection of the money is due on January 31, 2015.

### Explanation:

Just as we have explained before, the two transactions would have been analyzed by firstly examining the source documents and determining the accounts affected. These documents are the two invoices indicating the services provided totaling $2,000 to which we are expecting to collect the money earned at a later date. Therefore, we would have some service revenue plus the expectation of receiving the same amount of cash by January 31$^{st}$ which represents our receivables.

After analyzing the transactions, we now use the double entry system of accounting to record the transactions in the journal by debiting accounts receivable and crediting service revenue as shown below.

**Journal**

| Date | Account title & explanation | Debit | Credit |
|---|---|---|---|
| 01/01/2015 | Accounts receivable-Company Y | 980 | |
| | Service revenue | | 980 |
| | *To record tax accounting services provided on credit.* | | |
| | Accounts receivable-Company Z | 1,020 | |
| | Service revenue | | 1,020 |
| | *To record tax accounting services provided on credit.* | | |

Based on this example, the next step is to post the entries to the Accounts Receivable Ledger (Subsidiary Ledger) by debiting the respective customer account with the amount they each owe.

### Accounts Receivable Ledger

**Company Y**

| Date | Debit | Credit | Balance |
|---|---|---|---|
| 01/01/2015 | 980 | | 980 |

**Company Z**

| Date | Debit | Credit | Balance |
|---|---|---|---|
| 01/01/2015 | 1,020 | | 1,020 |

The final step is to transfer the total from the Accounts Receivable Ledger to the General Ledger. Remember that the Accounts Receivable account in the general ledger now acts as the control account for the accounts receivable (subsidiary) ledger.

### General Ledger

**Accounts receivable**

| Date | Debit | Credit | Balance |
|---|---|---|---|
| 01/01/2015 | 2,000 | | 2,000 |

**Tax Acc. Service Revenue**

| Date | Debit | Credit | Balance |
|---|---|---|---|
| 01/01/2015 | | 2,000 | (2,000) |

**Note that, if payment is collected from Company Y on the due date 01/31/2015, then the entries to record and post the collection will be as follow:**

## Journal

| Date | Account title & explanation | Debit | Credit |
|---|---|---|---|
| 01/31/2015 | Cash | 980 | |
| | Accounts Receivable-Company Y | | 980 |
| | *To record payment collected from customer.* | | |

### Accounts Receivable Ledger

#### Company Y

| Date | Debit | Credit | Balance |
|---|---|---|---|
| 01/01/2015 | 980 | | 980 |
| 01/31/2015 | | 980 | 0 |

#### Company Z

| Date | Debit | Credit | Balance |
|---|---|---|---|
| 01/01/2015 | 1,020 | | 1,020 |

### General Ledger

#### Accounts receivable

| Date | Debit | Credit | Balance |
|---|---|---|---|
| 01/01/2015 | 2,000 | | 2,000 |
| 01/31/2015 | | 980 | 1,020 |

Note that, if you are using an accounting software then all you need to do is enter the information from the relevant invoices/checks and the software does the rest of the transactions behind the scene. However, the above explanation should provide you with an understanding of the manual approach.

# Credit balance in accounts receivable

While it is the norm for accounts receivable to have a debit balance, there are times when at least one customer account has a credit balance. This credit balance can occur, for example; the customer makes an overpayment or return of merchandise after payment. Whenever this happens, it should *not* be used to offset against the accounts with debit balances but listed separately as a liability named *credit balance in customer's account* on the balance sheet.

## Lock Box Banking

Instead of allowing the customers to remit check payments to the company, the payments can be directed to a special post office box that the company's bank can access. The checks are then collected and deposited to the company's bank account by an officer from the bank. This procedure allows the deposit of the checks in the company's bank account on a timely basis.

# Handling Discount

**Trade discount**

There are times when the seller offers a trade discount if the purchaser buys a large quantity (bulk purchase) and these transactions mostly happen in certain situations. For example, Company A sells a single item for $112 but gives a trade discount of $12 if you purchase a quantity of 200 or more.

**Sales discount/Cash discount**

When the seller makes a sale, he/she gives a discount (sales discount) to the buyer so as to encourage him/her to pay early. If accepted, the buyer gets a reduction in the purchase price. The discount is part of the payment terms listed on the invoice sometimes as 2/10, n 30. Meaning that, the buyer has 30 days within the invoice date to pay the total on the invoice, but gets a 2% discount if paid within 10 days of the invoice date. (Zero discount if paid on the 11$^{th}$ to the 30$^{th}$ day of the invoice date).

Buyers who missed the discount period will likely to pay their invoices close to the 30$^{th}$ day of the invoice date.

2/10, E.O.M., net 30, E.O.M. means 2% discount if paid within ten days of the following month or full payment by the 30$^{th}$ day of the following month.

## Illustration V11

For example, Premier Business Services provided tax preparation service and sent an invoice dated 03/01/2015 to Company X for $810 and outlined on the invoice that the payment term is 2/10, n 30.

**Premier Business Services**  **INVOICE: 010**

Street Address, City, State  March 01, 2015
Phone: 888-888-8888 | Fax: 555-555-5555
www.premaddress.com

**TO:**
Company X
Street Address, City, State
Phone: 999-999-9999 | Fax: 666-666-6666
www.comaddress.com

| P.O. Number | | | | | | Terms |
|---|---|---|---|---|---|---|
| 008 | | | | | | 2/10, n30 |
| Quantity | Description | | | Unit Price | | Total |
| 1 | To prepare tax return for the year 2014 | | | | | 810 |
| | | | | | | |

Make all checks payable to Premier Business Services

**THANK YOU FOR YOUR BUSINESS!**

If payment is received by Premier within the ten days as outlined on the invoice, then the amount collected would be $794 which is $810 - (2% x 810).

Note that, the paying companies at most times are happy to utilize the benefit of any discount received since the amount saved over any period can be substantial.

There are two ways a company can record this type of transaction: (1) The Gross Method and (2) The Net Method.

With the above example, Premier has the option to record it as follows:

**Gross method - On the issue date of the invoice:**

### Journal

| Date | Account title & explanation | Debit | Credit |
|---|---|---|---|
| 03/01/2015 | Accounts Receivable-Company X | 810 | |
| | Service Revenue | | 810 |
| | *To record tax preparation service at gross amount.* | | |
| **If the payment is received within the discount period** | | | |
| 03/10/2015 | Cash | 794 | |
| | Sales discount | 16 | |
| | Accounts Receivable-Company X | | 810 |
| | *To record collection of cash minus the discount.* | | |
| **If the payment is received after the discount period** | | | |
| 03/31/2015 | Cash | 810 | |
| | Accounts Receivable-Company X | | 810 |
| | *To record collection of cash.* | | |

## Net method - On the issue date of the invoice:

### Journal

| Date | Account title & explanation | Debit | Credit |
|---|---|---|---|
| 03/01/2015 | Accounts Receivable-Company X | 794 | |
| | Service Revenue | | 794 |
| | *To record tax preparation service at net amount.* | | |

**If the payment is received within the discount period**

| | | | |
|---|---|---|---|
| 03/10/2015 | Cash | 794 | |
| | Accounts Receivable-Company X | | 794 |
| | *To record collection of cash.* | | |

**If the payment is received after the discount period**

| | | | |
|---|---|---|---|
| 03/31/2015 | Accounts Receivable-Company X | 16 | |
| | Sales discount forfeited | | 16 |
| | *To record sales discount forfeited.* | | |
| 03/31/2015 | Cash | 810 | |
| | Accounts Receivable-Company X | | 810 |
| | *To record collection of cash.* | | |

We need to bear in mind that if the company uses the gross method, then **there is a** need to make an estimate of potential sales discount for transactions close to the end of the accounting period. This estimate is in view of the fact that the company expects the customers taking sales discount against outstanding accounts receivables. On the other hand, if the company uses the net method, then there is the need to make an appropriate estimation for Sales Discount Forfeited. This forfeiture becomes part of **Other Revenue.**

## Merchandise Inventory Sales

With the sale of merchandise, there can be a difference regarding the journal entries involved. If the company is using the *perpetual inventory system,* then there is a need to record two separate sets of journal entries to facilitate the transaction. The first one is to recognize the revenue from the sale, and the other is to recognize the cost of the inventory. These recordings are done in the journal whether the sale is cash or credit. Alternatively, if the company is using the *periodic inventory system*, then only a single journal entry is needed to record the revenue effect on the date of sale.

*The perpetual inventory system* is the opposite of *the periodic inventory system.* The perpetual is the keeping of continuous update to the inventory records regarding sales, purchases or return of merchandise inventories. While the periodic as the name suggests, the update is done to the merchandise inventory records periodically.

### Illustration V111

#### Sale of merchandise with discount

Let us assume that JOAH Trading sold $5,000 worth of merchandise on credit on 02/01/2015 with a term of 2/10, n 30. The merchandise had a cost of $3,000.

Recorded using the Gross method - Perpetual (two entries are needed on the date of sale to record the revenue and cost of goods sold effect).

## Journal

| Date | Account title & explanation | Debit | Credit |
|---|---|---|---|
| 02/01/2015 | Accounts Receivable | 5,000 | |
| | Sales Revenue | | 5,000 |
| | *To record merchandise sold on credit.* | | |
| 02/01/2015 | Cost of goods sold | 3,000 | |
| | Merchandise Inventory | | 3,000 |
| | *To record the cost of merchandise sold.* | | |

If the customer decides to pay the invoice by 02/10/2015, JOAH records the receipt of the payment as:

## Journal

| Date | Account title & explanation | Debit | Credit |
|---|---|---|---|
| 02/10/2015 | Cash | 4,900 | |
| | Sales Discount | 100 | |
| | (5000x2%) | | |
| | Accounts Receivable | | 5,000 |
| | *To record receipt of the payment.* | | |

Note that, if receipt of payment is after 02/10/2015, then there is no discount.

Recorded using the Gross method - Periodic (only the entry to show the revenue effect needed on the date of sale).

**Journal**

| Date | Account title & explanation | Debit | Credit |
|---|---|---|---|
| 02/01/2015 | Accounts Receivable | 5,000 | |
| | Sales Revenue | | 5,000 |
| | *To record merchandise sold on credit.* | | |

If the customer decides to pay the invoice by 02/10/2015, JOAH records the receipt of the payment as: (**Same as perpetual**)

**Journal**

| Date | Account title & explanation | Debit | Credit |
|---|---|---|---|
| 02/10/2015 | Cash | 4,900 | |
| | Sales Discount | 100 | |
| | (5000x2%) | | |
| | Accounts Receivable | | 5,000 |
| | *To record receipt of the payment.* | | |

**Note that, if payment is received after 02/10/2015, then there is no discount.**

# Analysis of Accounts Receivable

Since accounts receivable sometimes total close to one-month sale for most businesses that offer credit sales, it is of great importance that management pays close attention to the balance at least on a monthly basis.

While we are aware that there is always a balance in the accounts receivable for these businesses, many of them try to offer the customers a cash discount to encourage then to pay early. The cash discount is sometimes 2% if paid within ten days of the date of invoice.

Some customers make many purchases within a month and hence receiving an invoice for each purchase. Instead of asking these customers to make out a check for each of these invoices, an arrangement could be agreed upon to let these customers group all invoices for any particular month and make out one check by the 10$^{th}$ of the following month and still enjoy the 2% discount.

An important point to note is that invoices made out closer to the end of the month would be captured for payment just closer to 10 days of the normal discount period while those made out early in the month would enjoy a payment period of more than 30 days and still be benefitting from the 2% discount.

Management can use the following reports to assess the status of the accounts receivable position of their company (**Assume that all sales are on credit**):

## A/R report on December 31, 2015

|  | December 2015 | November 2015 |
|---|---|---|
| Accounts receivable balance | 434,600 | 527,875 |
| Cash collection | 503,275 | 518,000 |
| Net sales for the month | 410,000 | 515,000 |

| | |
|---|---|
| Current accounts receivable balance to current sales (434.6/410)100 | 106% |
| December cash collected to November sales (503.275/515)100 | 98% |
| December cash collected to November A/R bal. (503.275/527.875)100 | 95% |

The 106% tells us immediately that accounts receivable for the month of December 2015 are 6% more than the month's sales of $410,000.

**Note that, the November's accounts receivable balance of 527,875 minus the December's cash collection of 503,275 = 24,600 would have been overdue after the end of December 2015.**

### Aging of past due accounts report

| Past due | Total Amount | % to current A/R balance |
|---|---|---|
| 1 to 30 days | 10,865 | 2.5% |
| 31 to 60 days | 6,519 | 1.5% |
| 61 to 90 days | 4,346 | 1% |
| 91 days and more | 2,870 | .66% |
| | 24,600 | 5.66% |

This report provides management with an insight with regards to the **past due** amount of accounts receivable. All efforts should be made to keep this number within the company's expectation. (The amount of $24,600 is 5.66% of the total A/R balance for December 2015 that has passed the due date of the receivables).

Please be aware that this report can be done for an entire year instead of just for two months.

**Alternatively,** another form of receivables analysis is examining the Days' Sales Outstanding (DSO) or the Average Collection Period (ACP) along with the average daily sales (ADS).

**Note that, the DSO or ACP is simply a ratio that tells us the average number of days a company takes to collect its money from customers after the creation of the accounts receivable. This ratio provides us with an idea as to how quickly a company is collecting its accounts receivable. Which means the faster the company collects its receivables, the better it is for the company.**

The Average Daily Sales (ADS) is the average sales made per day.

It is good to point out at this time that accounts receivable (A/R) is equal to the DSO or the ACP multiplied by the average daily sales.

## Illustration 1X

Keeping it simple by assuming that the **sales made are on credit** and payments are received on the last day of the discount period (the tenth of the month) or the thirtieth of the month.

JOAH Trading started operation on January 1, 2015, and selling merchandise on a 2/10, n 30 credit period. Each day of sales $2,000. At the end of the first ten days, total receivables is $20,000. (2,000x10).

Now assume that the total sales for the year is $2,000,000 and 60% of the customers utilized the discount by paying on the tenth of the month and the remaining 40% paid by the thirtieth.

JOAH Trading's DSO would be: 0.6 (10) + 0.4 (30) = 18 days (Number of days the company takes to collect its money)

JOAH Trading's ADS would be: Annual Sales/365 = 2,000,000/365 = $5,479

Total accounts receivable = 18 x 5,479 = $98,622

If you only had JOAH Trading's financial statements with accounts receivable balance and total sales for the year, the Days' Sales Outstanding (DSO) would also be as follows:

Accounts receivable/Average Daily Sales = 98,622/5,479 = 18 days.

When analyzing the Days' Sales Outstanding, if the established credit period for the company is 30 days but the DSO when calculated is proven to be 46 days, the result is that it is taking 16 days more than the credit period to collect the receivables.

**Now, let's assume the collection of the entire receivables is within 60 days.**

**Aging Schedule**

JOAH Trading

| Age of Accounts # of days | Value of account | Percentage of Total value |
|---|---|---|
| 0 – 10 | 9,862 | 10 |
| 10 – 30 | 14,793 | 15 |
| 31 – 45 | 29,587 | 30 |
| 46 – 60 | <u>44,380</u> | <u>45</u> |
|  | <u>98,622</u> | <u>100</u> |

Our computation would be: 0.1 (10) + 0.15 (30) + 0.3 (45) + 0.45 (60) = 46 days. This example is good for a 60-day credit period.

If JOAH Trading had not collected the entire receivables within the 30 days established credit period according to the following aging schedule:

**Aging Schedule**

JOAH Trading

| Age of Accounts # of days | Value of account | Percentage of Total value |
|---|---|---|
| 0 – 10 | 29,587 | 30 |
| 10 – 30 | 39,449 | 40 |
| 31 – 45 | 14,793 | 15 |
| 46 – 60 | 9,862 | 10 |
| Over 60 days | <u>4,931</u> | <u>5</u> |
|  | <u>98,622</u> | <u>100</u> |

It means that 30% (the 31-45 days 15% + 46-60 days 10% + over 60 days 5%) of the receivables are past due.

# Sales Returns and Allowances

Let us now shift our focus to see how we would handle issues that relate to sales returns and allowances, but before we do so, there is a need to understand the meaning of these transaction types.

**Sales Returns-** This occurs when the customer returns the merchandise to the seller after the execution of a sale.

**Sales Allowances-** This occurs when the goods sold to a customer are discovered to be damaged or defective, and the customer is willing to keep them for a reduced price.

There are three instances when a customer might make a return of merchandise:

1. Before payment of the invoice.
2. After payment of the invoice and the discount was taken
3. After payment of the invoice and no discount was taken

## Sales returns

### Illustration X

**Return of the merchandise before payment of the invoice - Perpetual**

Assume that after JOAH Trading had made a credit sale on 3/01/2015 for $12,500, the cost of goods sold $5,000, term 2/10, n 30, the customer returned part of the merchandise that was sold for $500 and cost $200 on 03/05/2015.

Again, based on the **perpetual system** of how we record inventories, there is a need to have two sets of journal entries.

**The first one would be to record the reduction in the accounts receivable and to establish the sales returns as a reduction in sales.**

### Journal

| Date | Account title & explanation | Debit | Credit |
|---|---|---|---|
| 03/05/2015 | Sales return and allowances | 500 | |
| | Accounts Receivable | | 500 |
| | *To record sales returns.* | | |

The accounts receivable ledger will now show a reduced balance of $12,000. This is indicated below.

### Accounts Receivable Ledger

| Date | Debit | Credit | Balance |
|---|---|---|---|
| 03/01/2015 | 12,500 | | 12,500 |
| 03/05/2015 | | 500 | 12,000 |

Once the returned goods can be re-sold, **the second journal entry** is to record the return of the goods to the warehouse by effecting the increased change to the merchandise inventory account and reducing the cost of goods sold.

## Journal

| Date | Account title & explanation | Debit | Credit |
|---|---|---|---|
| 03/05/2015 | Merchandise inventory | 200 | |
| | Cost of goods sold | | 200 |
| | *To record the return of goods added to inventory.* | | |

Note that, the *above* transaction would *only* occur if the merchandise returned is in good condition. If the returned merchandise is defective, and the estimated value is $130, then JOAH would make the following journal entry:

## Journal

| Date | Account title & explanation | Debit | Credit |
|---|---|---|---|
| 03/05/2015 | Merchandise inventory | 130 | |
| | Loss from defective merchandise | 70 | |
| | Cost of goods sold | | 200 |
| | *To record the return of defective goods added to inventory.* | | |

*Note: Under the periodic, only one entry (see below).*

## Journal

| Date | Account title & explanation | Debit | Credit |
|---|---|---|---|
| 03/05/2015 | Sales return and allowances | 500 | |
| | Accounts Receivable | | 500 |
| | *To record sales returns.* | | |

## Return of the merchandise after the payment of the invoice and the customer already took the discount -Perpetual

## Illustration X1

Assume that the customer returned merchandise inventory that sold for $500 and cost $200 on 03/15/2015. Discount received was 2%.

**Journal**

| Date | Account title & explanation | Debit | Credit |
|---|---|---|---|
| 03/15/2015 | Sales returns and allowances | 490 | |
| | 500-(500x2%) | | |
| |     Accounts Receivable | | 490 |
| | *To record sales returns net of sales.* | | |

**Journal**

| Date | Account title & explanation | Debit | Credit |
|---|---|---|---|
| 03/15/2015 | Merchandise inventory | 200 | |
| |     Cost of goods sold | | 200 |
| | *To record the return of goods added to inventory.* | | |

Return of the merchandise after the payment of the invoice and the customer took no discount.

Note that, the journal entries would be the same as the case when the customer had returned the merchandise before payment of the invoice.

# Sales Allowances

With sales allowances, the journal entry is the same, except the second part that pertains to the merchandise inventory. Remember that in this scenario; the customer decided to keep the goods for a reduced price.

## Illustration X11

Assume that merchandise sold on account to the customer by JOAH Trading is discovered to be defective but the customer decided to keep it because JOAH offered a $600 reduction in the price before the customer takes the discount.

The journal entry to record this would be: (same for perpetual and periodic system of inventory).

**Journal**

| Date | Account title & explanation | Debit | Credit |
|---|---|---|---|
| 02/05/2015 | Sales returns and allowances | 600 | |
| | Accounts receivable | | 600 |
| | *To record sales allowances.* | | |

Note that, if the customer gets the allowance after they already made the payment, and took the discount, then the allowance would be net of $600 @ 2% which would be $588.

## Credit Memorandum

A credit memorandum is usually issued to the customer whenever there is a return or allowance. This memorandum informs the customer of the seller's credit to their account.

# Transportation Cost

There are times under the FOB shipping arrangement when the seller advances the transportation cost on behalf of the buyer and then includes it as part of the invoice sent to the customer.

## Illustration X111

Assume that on 01/01/2015, JOAH Trading sold $4,000 of merchandise on account to a customer and advanced the shipping cost of $200. The total of the invoice is $4,200. Term 2/10, n 30. The cost of the merchandise is $2,500. The perpetual system used.

The journal entries would be:

**Journal**

| Date | Account title & explanation | Debit | Credit |
|---|---|---|---|
| 01/01/2015 | Accounts receivable | 4,000 | |
| | Sales revenue | | 4,000 |
| | *To record sales made on account.* | | |
| | Accounts receivable | 200 | |
| | Cash | | 200 |
| | *To record transportation cost.* | | |
| | Cost of goods sold | 2,500 | |
| | Merchandise Inventory | | 2,500 |
| | *To record cost of merchandise sold.* | | |

On 01/10/2015, JOAH received payment from the customer for sale made on 01/01/2015 less discount of 2%.

**Journal**

| Date | Account title & explanation | Debit | Credit |
|---|---|---|---|
| 01/10/2015 | Cash | 4,120 | |
| | Sales Discount | 80 | |
| | (4,000x2%) | | |
| | Accounts Receivable | | 4,200 |
| | *To record receipt of the payment.* | | |

# Valuing Accounts Receivable

This is a good time to realize that the money owed to us (receivable) for the value of the goods we sold or services rendered on **credit** will very likely not collected in full.

For example, if Premier Business Services has a total of $1,225 worth of receivables and is planning to collect it at some future date, there is a strong possibility that some of these customers might not pay. Therefore, Premier may only collect $1,000 and then has to treat the remaining $225 as uncollectible. Because of this uncertainty, the real value of the receivables has to be adjusted downward by the $225. In this case, the value of the receivables would be $1,000 which is equal to the net realizable value. The collection expected is $1,000.

**It is also important to note that if the creation of the receivables is from the sale of merchandise inventory, it can also be further reduced by any returns or allowances.**

**Please pay careful attention:** Since we have now realized that the chance for us to collect all of the receivables outstanding is very unlikely, there are two methods that companies use to record this **uncollectible amount. Bad debt is the name given to the uncollectible amount.** They are the direct write-off method and the allowance method.

The time to make the adjustment on the receivables normally occurs at the **end of the accounting period** but the write-off of the doubtful accounts can also occur within the period.

**Direct Write-Off Method:** Under this method, companies **do not** make an entry on the books **until they have identified** the specific amount as uncollectible.

## Illustration X1V

If Premier Business Services on December 31, 2014, has accounts receivable of $1,000 and realizes that $225 is uncollectible because the customer is bankrupt or insolvent, it then chooses to reduce the receivables by performing the following entries:

### Journal

| Date | Account title & explanation | Debit | Credit |
|---|---|---|---|
| 12/31/2014 | Bad Debt Expense | 255 | |
| | Accounts receivable | | 255 |
| | *To record write off of uncollectible account.* | | |

### Ledger
### Bad Debt Expense

| Date | | Debit | Credit | Balance |
|---|---|---|---|---|
| 12/31/2014 | | 225 | | 225 |

### Accounts Receivable Ledger

| Date | | Debit | Credit | Balance |
|---|---|---|---|---|
| 12/31/2014 | | 1,000 | | 1,000 |
| 12/31/2014 | | | 225 | 775 |

# Bad Debt Recovered

There are times when there is a recovery at a later date of the amount previously written off. This recovery is sometimes due to the additional effort placed on the customers for them to pay.

Example: If Premier had written off the $225 on 12/31/2014, and the customer is now in a position to settle the debt, we re-establish the amount by reversing the transaction. The following book entries are necessary:

**Journal**

| Date | Account titles & explanation | Debit | Credit |
|---|---|---|---|
| 01/31/2015 | Accounts receivable | 225 | |
| | Bad Debt Expense | | 225 |
| | *To record the reinstatement of account previously written off.* | | |

**Accounts Receivable Ledger**

| Date | Debit | Credit | Balance |
|---|---|---|---|
| 12/31/2014 | 1,000 | | 1,000 |
| 12/31/2014 | | 225 | 775 |
| 01/31/2015 | 225 | | 1,000 |

**General Ledger**
**Bad Debt Expense**

| Date | Debit | Credit | Balance |
|---|---|---|---|
| 01/31/2015 | | 225 | (225) |

Premier makes the following entries for the cash collection:

### Journal

| Date | Account titles & explanation | Debit | Credit |
|---|---|---|---|
| 1/31/2015 | Cash | 225 | |
| | Accounts receivable | | 225 |
| | To record the collection of the payment. | | |

### Accounts Receivable Ledger

| Date | Debit | Credit | Balance |
|---|---|---|---|
| 12/31/2014 | 1,000 | | 1,000 |
| 12/31/2014 | | 225 | 775 |
| 01/31/2015 | 225 | | 1,000 |
| 01/31/2015 | | 225 | 775 |

**Note that, sometimes the reinstatement of the account is only made based on the recovery of a partial amount; if this is the case, then you can treat it according to the amount received.**

**There are some things to note about the direct write-off method:**

Firstly, it is not GAAP. It is preferably used for tax purposes because the Tax Authority does not want you to take a write off until you are sure that there is no collection of the amount. The direct write-off at most times fails to match the period of the sale; critics complain that it is deficient. That is, the company might have made the sale (revenue) in the fiscal year of 2013, but the write-off (expense) doesn't occur until sometime in 2014. Therefore, the expense would not match the revenue (The Matching Principle) in the same period and hence failing to satisfy the principle of matching revenue with the expense.

**The Matching Principle:** This is a principle of accounting where under Generally Accepted Accounting Principle (GAAP); companies match their expense to the period it helped to create the revenue.

Using the direct write-off method is good in situations when the amount uncollectible is immaterial.

Immaterial, in this case, means that the uncollectible amount has little or no effect on the users of the financial statements.

**The Allowance Method:** This is the second method that companies use to record the uncollectible amount of accounts receivable. This method relies on estimation, and it is GAAP. Under this method, companies make an estimate of the amount of the receivable that is uncollectible. They are also able to match the bad debt expense with the revenue it enabled.

There are two approaches used to estimate the uncollectible as bad debt expense under the Allowance Method. One entails a percentage estimate of the total receivables on hand, and the other involves a percentage estimate of the total credit sales for the accounting period. These estimations are used to make an adjustment to the total receivables at the **end of the accounting period.**

**Percent of total receivables/ Balance sheet method:** There are two ways to make an estimation of the amount of uncollectible under this method.

1) Use a composite rate for calculating the uncollectible on the total receivables.
2) Set up an aging schedule of the accounts receivable (a schedule based on the age of each receivable). Then apply an individual rate to each age group.

Please note your experience or your understanding of the industry your company is operating within can help you in determining a rate.

## Illustration XV

Let us examine an example using the composite rate method of estimation. Assume that Premier Business Services has a total $52,200 worth of receivables on December 31, 2014. The management estimated a non-collection of 5% of this amount.

That is 5% of 52,200 = 2,610

**The book entries would be:**

### Journal

| Date | Account Titles and Explanation | Debit | Credit |
|---|---|---|---|
| 12/31/2014 | Bad debt expense | 2,610 | |
| | Allowance for doubtful accounts | | 2,610 |
| | *To make an allowance for amount uncollectible.* | | |

### General Ledger
### Bad Debt Expense

| Date | Debit | Credit | Balance |
|---|---|---|---|
| 12/31/2014 | 2,610 | | 2,610 |

### Allowance for doubtful accounts

| Date | Debit | Credit | Balance |
|---|---|---|---|
| 12/31/2014 | | 2,610 | (2,610) |

An extract from the balance sheet:

**Premier Business Services**
**Balance Sheet at 12/31/2014**

**Current Account**

| | | |
|---|---|---|
| Accounts receivable | 52,200 | |
| Allowance for doubtful accounts | (2,610) | |
| Net accounts receivable | | 49,590 |

Note that, the amount representing allowance for doubtful accounts on the balance sheet is a *Contra Asset*. That is, it reduces the amount in accounts receivable.

## Illustration XVI

Now for an example using the aging of receivables method: Assume that the amount of receivables outstanding is $55,659 on December 31, 2014.

You would construct a schedule for example as shown below:

**Premier Business Services**
**Schedule of Accounts Receivable by age**
**December 31, 2014**

| Customers | Total | Under 60 days | 60-90 days | 91-120 days | Over 120 days |
|---|---|---|---|---|---|
| John Brown | $ 7,272 | 7,272 | | | |
| Andrew Richards | 6,077 | 5,121 | 956 | | |
| Ted Thompson | 9,322 | 3,157 | 2,534 | 3,631 | |
| Sharon Green | 8,333 | 5,234 | | | 3,099 |

| | | | | | |
|---|---|---|---|---|---|
| Pamela Stone | 10,521 | 8,147 | | 2,374 | |
| Rebecca Horne | 1,254 | | | | 1,254 |
| Gretchel Coombs | 12,880 | 10,571 | 2,309 | | |
| | 55,659 | 39,502 | 5,799 | 9,104 | 1,254 |
| | ====== | ===== | ===== | ===== | ===== |

| Age | Amount | Uncollectible Percentage estimated | Dollar amount uncollectible |
|---|---|---|---|
| Under 60 days | 39,502 | 4% | 1,580 |
| 60-90 days | 5,799 | 10% | 580 |
| 91-120 days | 9,104 | 15% | 1,366 |
| Over 120 days | 1,254 | 20% | 251 |

Total amount of allowance for doubtful accounts 12/31/2014     3,777

## Journal

| Date | Account titles and explanation | Debit | Credit |
|---|---|---|---|
| 12/31/2014 | Bad debt expense | 3,777 | |
| | Allowance for doubtful accounts | | 3,777 |
| | *To make an allowance for amount uncollectible.* | | |

An extract from the balance sheet:

**Premier Business Services**
**Balance Sheet at 12/31/2014**

**Current Account**

| | |
|---|---|
| Accounts receivable | 55,659 |
| Allowance for doubtful accounts | (3,777) |
| Net accounts receivable | 51,882 |

**Percent of sales /Income statement approach:** The use of this method focuses only on the fact that there is a likelihood for a non-collection of a percentage of the credit sales made for a particular period.

## Illustration XV11

Premier Business Services made credit sales totaling $332,000 for the period January 01, 2014 - December 31, 2014. Based on management experience and understanding of the industry the Company is operating within, they make an estimate that 2% of the credit sales is uncollectible. That is 332,000 x 2% = 6,640.

This is an adjusting entry being made at the end of an accounting period:

### Journal

| Date | Account titles and explanation | Debit | Credit |
|---|---|---|---|
| 12/31/2014 | Bad debt expense | 6,640 | |
| | Allowance for doubtful accounts | | 6,640 |
| | *To make an allowance for amount uncollectible.* | | |

**Writing off a bad debt under the allowance method:** There are times when management has realized that the money owed by a particular customer is no longer doubtful. The amount owed seems uncollectible, either because the customer has become bankrupt or has been experiencing some other difficulty.

With this realization in mind, management has now decided to remove the amount owed or the customer from the books by reducing the allowance for doubtful accounts.

This is done by debiting the allowance for doubtful accounts and crediting accounts receivable.

## Illustration XV111

The management of Premier Business Services decided on 06/30/2015, that the account belonging to Rebecca Horne is uncollectible after numerous efforts of trying to collect. As a result of this, they have decided to write off the amount owed by removing it from the books.

| Date | Account titles and explanation | Debit | Credit |
|---|---|---|---|
| 06/30/2015 | Allowance for doubtful accounts | 1,254 | |
| | Accounts receivable-Rebecca Horne | | 1,254 |
| | *To record write-off of doubtful amount- Rebecca Horne.* | | |

### General Ledger
### Accounts Receivable

| Date | Debit | Credit | Balance |
|---|---|---|---|
| 12/31/2014 | 55,659 | | 55,659 |
| 06/30/2015 | | 1,254 | 54,405 |

### Allowance for doubtful accounts

| Date | Debit | Credit | Balance |
|---|---|---|---|
| 12/31/2014 | | 3,777 | (3,777) |
| 06/30/2015 | 1,254 | | (2,523) |

Note that, this entry does not affect your income statement, net realizable value of accounts receivable nor total assets because the credited amount to the accounts receivable is equal to the amount debited to the allowance for doubtful accounts which is a contra-asset account.

The non-change in the net accounts receivable on the balance sheet is shown below.

## Before the write-off:

**Premier Business Services**
**Balance sheet at 12/31/2014**

### Current Account

| | | |
|---|---:|---:|
| Accounts receivable | 55,659 | |
| Allowance for doubtful accounts | (3,777) | |
| Net accounts receivable | | 51,882 |

## After the write-off:

**Premier Business Services**
**Balance sheet at 06/30/2015**

### Current Account

| | | |
|---|---:|---:|
| Accounts receivable | 54,405 | |
| Allowance for doubtful accounts | (2,523) | |
| Net accounts receivable | | 51,882 |

Note: Do not confuse the writing-off of doubtful accounts with the direct write-off method.

Under the write-off of doubtful accounts, the net accounts receivable will not change, but under the direct write-off method, there is a change in net accounts receivable.

### Prior year balance in Allowance for doubtful accounts

Once the company is in its second year or more of operation, at most times, there is a beginning balance in the allowance for doubtful accounts. This amount can be a debit or credit balance.

## Prior credit balance in the allowance for doubtful accounts

Remember that under the percentage of receivables method, the balance in this account is continuous. That means, if the accounts receivable balance should increase in its second year when compared to its first year, then there would be an increase of the ending balance in the doubtful accounts.

## Illustration X1X

If the accounts receivable had a balance of $50,000 on 12/31/2014, with a 5% uncollectible, the following would happened.

50,000 X 5% = 2,500

Let us use a T-Account for this representation

| Accounts receivable | | Allowance for doubtful accounts | |
|---|---|---|---|
| 12/31/2014   50,000 | | | 12/31/2014   2,500 |

The balance in accounts receivable on 12/31/2015 is now $60,000, then the change would now be: 60,000 X 5% = 3,000

| Accounts receivable | | Allowance for doubtful accounts | |
|---|---|---|---|
| 12/31/2015   60,000 | | | 12/31/2014   2,500 |
| | | | 12/31/2015   500 |
| | | | -------- |
| | | | 12/31/2015   3,000 |
| | | | ===== |

Note that, the $500 represents the amount of bad debt expense for 2015 because of the increase in accounts receivable from $50,000 to $60,000.

### Journal

| Date | Account titles and explanation | Debit | Credit |
|---|---|---|---|
| 12/31/2015 | Bad debt expense | 500 | |
| | Allowance for doubtful accounts | | 500 |
| | *To make an allowance for amount uncollectible.* | | |

Let us look at another scenario; if on 06/30/2015, there were $1,500 of doubtful accounts that were considered as uncollectible (write-off) and the accounts receivable balance on 12/31/2015, is $60,000, then the following would happen:

| Accounts receivable | | Allowance for doubtful accounts | |
|---|---|---|---|
| | | 12/31/2014 | 2,500 |
| 06/30/2015  1,500 | | | |
| | 06/30/2015  1,500 | | |
| | | Bal. 06/30/15 | 1,000 |
| 12/31/2015  60,000 | | 12/31/2015 | 2,000 |
| | | | -------- |
| | | 12/31/2015 | 3,000 |
| | | | ===== |

## Allowance for doubtful accounts

| | | |
|---|---|---|
| Credit balance | 12/31/2014 | $2,500 |
| Amount debited | 06/30/2015 | <u>1,500</u> |
| Credit balance | 06/30/2015 | 1,000 |
| Amount credited | 12/31/2015 | <u>2,000</u> |
| Ending credit bal. | 12/31/2015 | 3,000* |
| | | ====== |

*$60,000 x 5% = 3,000

Note that, the balance in the allowance for doubtful accounts has to equal to the decided percentage amount of the receivables. In our example, we used 5%.

### Journal

| Date | Account titles and explanation | Debit | Credit |
|---|---|---|---|
| 06/30/2015 | Allowance for doubtful accounts | 1,500 | |
| | Accounts receivable | | 1,500 |
| | *To record write-off of doubtful accounts.* | | |
| | | | |
| 12/31/2015 | Bad debt expense | 2,000 | |
| | Allowance for doubtful accounts | | 2,000 |
| | *To record estimate for doubtful accounts.* | | |

## Prior debit balance in the Allowance for doubtful accounts

There are instances when the amount of allowance for doubtful accounts written-off during a period exceeds the amount previously estimated and causes the balance in the allowance for doubtful accounts to be a debit balance instead of the normal credit balance. Whenever this happens, it means that the amount estimated as allowance for doubtful accounts was insufficient.

## Illustration XX

If on 12/31/2014, the accounts receivable balance were $50,000 and an estimation that there is a 5% non-collection of the receivables. The setting up of the following accounts:

| Accounts receivable | | Allowance for doubtful accounts | |
|---|---|---|---|
| 12/31/2014  50,000 | | | 12/31/2014  2,500 |

During the period it was discovered on 06/30/2015 that $3,000 of the accounts receivable were uncollectible (the doubtful amount of $2,500 plus an additional $500) and the accounts receivable balance on 12/31/2015 is $65,000, then the following would occur:

The entries are:

| Accounts receivable | | Allowance for doubtful accounts | |
|---|---|---|---|
| 12/31/2014  50,000 | | | 12/31/2014  2,500 |
| | 06/30/2015  3000 | 06/30/2015  3,000 | |
| | | Bal. 06/30/15  500 | |
| | | | 12/31/2015  3,750 |
| | | | -------- |
| | | Bal | |
| | | 12/31/2015  3,250 | |
| | | ===== | |

| | |
|---|---|
| Credit balance of | $2,500 |
| Amount debited | 3,000 |
| Debit balance | 500 |
| Amount credited | 3,750 |
| Ending credit balance | 3,250* |
| | ====== |

*$65,000 x 5% = 3,250*

### Journal

| Date | Account titles and explanation | Debit | Credit |
|---|---|---|---|
| 06/30/2015 | Allowance for doubtful accounts | 3,000 | |
| | Accounts receivable | | 3,000 |
| | *To record write-off of doubtful accounts.* | | |

| Date | Account titles and explanation | Debit | Credit |
|---|---|---|---|
| 12/31/2015 | Bad debt expense | 3,750 | |
| | Allowance for doubtful accounts | | 3,750 |
| | *To record estimate for doubtful accounts.* | | |

## Recovering the bad debt previously written off

There are times after a customer account has been written off; they might try to restore their creditworthiness by paying a partial or the entire amount that was owed.

Whenever the payment is made, there are two accounting entries that you as a company need to make and they are:

1) The reversal of the transaction previously used to do the write-off by reinstating the account.
2) Show the collection of the cash collected from the account reinstated.

## Illustration XX1

On 01/31/2016, the customer Rebecca Horne has decided to pay the total amount of $1,254 owing to Premier Business Services.

**The first thing to do is reinstate Rebecca Horne's account.**

**Note:** Pay careful attention that the account credited is the allowance for doubtful accounts and not the bad debt account as in the case of the Direct Write-Off Method discussed earlier.

### Journal

| Date | Account titles and explanation | PR | Debit | Credit |
|---|---|---|---|---|
| 01/31/2016 | Accounts receivable-Rebecca Horne | | 1,254 | |
| | Allowance for doubtful accounts | | | 1,254 |
| | *To record the reinstatement of account previously written off.* | | | |

### General Ledger
### Accounts Receivable

| Date | Debit | Credit | Balance |
|---|---|---|---|
| 12/31/2014 | 55,659 | | 55,659 |
| 06/30/2015 | | 1,254 | 54,405 |
| 01/31/2016 | 1,254 | | 55,659 |

The second thing to do is record the collection of the cash paid by Rebecca Horne.

## Journal

| Date | Account titles and explanation | Debit | Credit |
|---|---|---|---|
| 01/31/2016 | Cash | 1,254 | |
| | Accounts receivable-Rebecca Horne | | 1,254 |
| | *To record the collection of the payment.* | | |

## General Ledger
### Accounts Receivable

| Date | Debit | Credit | Balance |
|---|---|---|---|
| 12/31/2014 | 55,659 | | 55,659 |
| 06/30/2015 | | 1,254 | 54,405 |
| 01/31/2016 | 1,254 | | 55,659 |
| 01/31/2016 | | 1,254 | 54,405 |

There are also times when the customer makes only a partial payment. Whenever this happens, the company has the option of reinstating the account in full if they believe the customer will eventually pay the full amount or just reinstate the account for the partial amount that the customer intends on paying.

## Illustration XX11

If Rebecca Horne had decided only to pay $800 of the amount owed, then the following is done:

**Journal**

| Date | Account titles and explanation | Debit | Credit |
|---|---|---|---|
| 01/31/2016 | Accounts receivable-Rebecca Horne | 800 | |
| | Allowance for doubtful accounts | | 800 |
| | *To record the reinstatement of partial amount previously written off.* | | |
| 01/31/2016 | Cash | 800 | |
| | Accounts receivable-Rebecca Horne | | 800 |
| | *To record the collection of the payment.* | | |

**Note that for simplicity, we kept the original balance of the accounts receivable from 12/31/2014 unchange so as to present the illustrations simple, but in the real world, the making of ongoing sales would have created a change in the balance throughout the period.**

# Credit Card Payments

Almost every company allows their customers to make purchases using some form of credit card. These credit cards are generally from a third party company such as Visa or MasterCard. Whenever the customer uses a credit card to make a payment, the selling company would then remit the credit card sales receipt electronically or manually to the credit card company to receive payment.

After the remittance of the sales receipt, the credit card company sometimes immediately makes the deposit of the sales amount less any fee charged or sometimes delays payment which in turn creates an account receivable.

In accounting for the receivable generated from the credit card transaction, we normally do the following:

### Illustration XX111

Let's assume that Premier Business Services provided service to a customer that pays by credit card of $500 on January 20, 2015, with a 3% fee. (The credit card company charges a fee).

Premier would then remit the credit card sales receipt electronically on the same day to the credit card company who in return might decide to settle the payment on January 23, 2015. The fact that the payment is not received immediately after the remittance, Premier would then make the following journal entry:

| Date | Account titles and explanation | Debit | Credit |
|---|---|---|---|
| 01/20/2015 | Accounts receivable- (Name of credit card Co.) | 485 | |
| | Credit card expense | 15 | |
| | Sales | | 500 |
| | *To record credit card sales.* | | |

If the cash is collected on January 23, then we make the following entry:

| Date | Account titles and explanation | Debit | Credit |
|---|---|---|---|
| 01/23/2015 | Cash | 485 | |
| | Accounts receivable - (Name of credit card Co.) | | 485 |

**Note that, if the selling company were a merchandising company then the transaction would have been the same except the additional entry of debit to cost of goods sold and the credit to merchandise inventory to account for the cost of the merchandise.**

# Sales in Foreign Currency

Premier Business Services conducts business at times with international clients. Some of these clients are allowed to pay on credit, and Premier is required to account for these credit sales.

If the customers are required to pay in US dollars, then regular accounts receivable is set up to accommodate the transactions.

Alternatively, if the sales transactions require the customers to pay in foreign currency, then a different approach is needed to handle the transactions.

## Illustration XX1V

If Premier Business Services did some consultancy work for a client in Europe on December 20, 2014, and it costed the client 2,000 Euros when the exchange rate was US$1.92 to 1 Euro. The client is paying the invoice on January 20, 2015.

Since Premier is a US based company who would maintain its record in US currency, there must be a conversion of the Euros to US dollars. Therefore, 2,000 X 1.92= 3,840.

The journal entry to record this transaction is:

| Date | Account titles and explanation | Debit | Credit |
|---|---|---|---|
| 12/20/2014 | Accounts receivable | 3,840 | |
| | Service Revenue | | 3,840 |
| | *To record sales revenue when the exchange rate was US$1.92 to 1 Euro.* | | |

On December 31, 2014, Premier prepares its year-end financial statements when the dollar $1.95 to 1 Euro.

Premier would have recognized a gain of $60.

2,000 x 1.95= 3,900
3,900-3,840= 60

| Date | Account titles and explanation | Debit | Credit |
|---|---|---|---|
| 31/12/2014 | Accounts Receivable | 60 | |
| | Gain on foreign exchange | | 60 |
| | *To record a gain based on the increase in value of the Euro since Dec. 20, 2014.* | | |

**Note that, the increase in the value of the Euro creates more US dollars upon conversion. Therefore, on December 31, 2014, 1 Euro is now equal to US$1.95.**

If on January 20, 2015, the due date of the invoice, the Euro continues to strengthen against the US dollar (1 Euro to US$1.97) then Premier would make the following entry:

2,000 x 1.97= 3,940
3,940-3,900= 40

| Date | Account titles and explanation | Debit | Credit |
|---|---|---|---|
| 01/20/2015 | Cash | 3,940 | |
| | Accounts receivable | | 3,900 |
| | Gain on foreign exchange | | 40 |

*To record receipt of 2000 Euros converted to dollars.*

Alternatively, if on the date of payment, the Euro weakens against the dollar to $1.85 then Premier would make the following entry:

2,000 x 1.85= 3,700
3,900- 3,700= 200

| Date | Account titles and explanation | Debit | Credit |
|---|---|---|---|
| 01/20/2015 | Cash | 3,700 | |
| | Loss on foreign exchange | 200 | |
| | Accounts receivable | | 3,900 |

*To record receipt of 2000 Euros converted to dollars.*

# Notes Receivable

**Promissory Note**

There has to be a **written promise** by someone to pay you a certain sum of money at a future date to make notes receivable. This description of a written promise is a *promissory note.* This written agreement can either be on a short or long-term basis for someone to receive or collect money at a future date.

**Note: Long term is a period greater than one year, while short term is a period within one year.**

A customer has put in writing a promise to pay Premier Business Services money at a definite future date. Therefore, in this scenario, the customer is the one who offered or issued the note, and Premier is the one who accepted or received the note.

One vital thing to pay attention to is that, because of the time value of money, all notes have an interest component to them whether they are *interest bearing* or *non-interest bearing.*

**The interest bearing notes** have a stated interest rate also referred to as the coupon or face rate.

**The non-interest bearing (zero-interest-bearing notes)** include an implicit interest rate as part of the face value.

These promissory notes are negotiable instruments and are somewhat liquid. Due to their fairly liquid feature, a holder can easily sell or trade the notes to receive cash. The usage of these notes forms part of many different types of transactions including paying for goods and services. These promissory notes also support the lending and borrowing of money. Companies can also use notes when doing business with customers who have poor credit rating.

Most companies prefer to accept a note from a customer because it provides them with an advantage in legal proceedings.

**Note that, for easy calculation; we are using 360 as the number of days per year and February with 28 days for calculation of interest.**

See below a sample of a promissory note

## Illustration XXV

---

**PROMISSORY NOTE**

**Date**

| Borrower's information: | Lender's information: |
|---|---|
| Name: | Name: |
| Address: | Address: |
| Date of birth: | Telephone #: |
| Social Security #: | Make check payable to: |

Loan amount:
Interest Rate:
Loan period:
Maturity date- I promise to pay on:


Signature of borrower or issuer of note:


Notary Public Seal:
Commission expired on:

---

Since the classification of notes receivable can either be short-term or long-term, we'll be examining each classification.

### Recognizing Short-term notes receivable

Short-term notes are mostly recorded at face value since they are generally not subjected to a premium or discount amortization.

Notes that are three months and under are generally cash equivalent. The issuer of the short-term note is obligated to pay the interest and the principal amount of the note at the maturity date.

## Illustration XXV1

Premier Business Services accepted a note receivable from a customer Barry Jones for services provided on January 15, 2015, of $2,000 with an interest rate of 10% settling in 90 days.

Recognizing this note on the date of service, Premier prepares the following journal entry:

### Journal

| Date | Account titles and explanation | Debit | Credit |
|---|---|---|---|
| 01/15/2015 | Notes Receivable | 2,000 | |
| | Service Revenue | | 2,000 |
| | *To record service provided in exchange for note.* | | |

### The honoring of the note

This is recorded in the journal as follows:

### Journal

| Date | Account titles and explanation | Debit | Credit |
|---|---|---|---|
| 04/15/2015 | Cash | 2,050 | |
| | Notes receivable | | 2,000 |
| | Interest revenue | | 50 |
| | (2,000 x 10% x 90/360) | | |
| | *To record the collection of note with interest.* | | |

The honoring of the note is on (January 15, 2015, plus 90 days) = April 15, 2015, which is the maturity date of the note.

Calculated as follows: 31 days in January minus January 15 the date of the note= 16 days. (16 days of January + 28 days of February + 31 days of March + 15 days of April) = 90 days.

On the date the note is honored, Premier receives interest revenue of $50 along with the principal amount of $2,000.

**The Balance Sheet effect:**

**Current Assets**
The Notes receivable        2,000

Once Premier Business Services has accepted the note, it appears as part of their current assets on the balance sheet as shown **above** and whenever honored or settled the principal portion converted to cash, plus an additional cash amount collected as interest revenue, shown **below** as balance sheet and income statement effect respectively.

**The Balance Sheet effect:**

**Current Assets**
Cash        2,050

**The Income Statement effect:**

**Revenue**
Interest revenue        50

## Conversion of accounts receivable to notes receivable

There are times when a customer needs additional time to settle their accounts receivable, and a note is used to substitute for the accounts receivable that are past due.

Note that, we can arrange for the conversion of accounts receivable to notes receivable so as to facilitate time extension on accounts that are past due.

Shown below is an example of this type of transaction:

## Illustration XXV11

Let us assume that on 12/31/2014, Premier Business Services has a customer with an outstanding amount owing of $800. The customer has decided to issue a 90 day, 9% notes to Premier for the $800.

Premier would record this as follows:

**Journal**

| Date | Account titles and explanation | Debit | Credit |
|---|---|---|---|
| 12/31/2014 | Notes Receivable | 800 | |
| | Accounts receivable | | 800 |
| | *To record the acceptance of a note for A/C receivable.* | | |

## The honoring of the note

Once the customer decided to settle the note at the end of the 90 days, the he/she would remit the full payment of the principal amount plus interest to Premier, who makes the following entry in their book.

### Journal

| Date | Account titles and explanation | Debit | Credit |
|---|---|---|---|
| 03/31/2015 | Cash | 818 | |
| | Notes receivable | | 800 |
| | Interest revenue | | 18 |
| | (800 x 9% x 90/360) | | |
| | To record the collection of note with interest. | | |

**Note that, there is a collection of the principal and interest at the maturity date for these short-term notes.**

**Balance Sheet effect: The Cash received of $818 is an addition to cash as part of current assets while the honoring of the note is a reduction of $800 to notes receivable-current assets.**

**Income Statement effect: The Interest Revenue of $18 increases the income which ultimately increases owner's equity.**

**The dishonoring of a note**

There are times after acceptance of a note from a customer, and the customer in return is unable to settle the note at the maturity date. Whenever an issue like this arises, the company changes the note receivable to an account receivable.

## Illustration XXV111

If Joe Brown a customer was unable to settle at the maturity date his 60 days, 9% note of $10,000 issued on January 01, 2015; then the following would happen.

The calculation of the interest revenue or interest earned would be:

10,000 x 9% x 60/360 = 150

**Journal**

| Date | Accounts titles and explanation | Debit | Credit |
|---|---|---|---|
| 03/02/2015 | Accounts receivable- Joe Brown | 10,150 | |
| | Interest Revenue | | 150 |
| | Notes receivable | | 10,000 |
| | *To record Joe Brown's dishonored note & interest earned.* | | |

### Accruals-end of period adjustment

At the end of the accounting period, sometimes there are notes outstanding, and because of this, there is a need to account for the accrued interest earned up to that time.

## Illustration XX1X

Premier Business Services took a $3,000, 90 days, 10% note on December 1, 2014, from a customer for services rendered. The fact that Premier's accounting period ends on December 31, 2014, there is a need to make a calculation at that time for the accrued interest earned during the period December 1 and December 31.

There is a need to make two entries:

The first one is to record the note accepted on December 01, 2014:

### Journal

| Date | Account titles and explanation | Debit | Credit |
|---|---|---|---|
| 12/01/2014 | Note receivable | 3,000 | |
| | Service revenue | | 3,000 |
| | *To record note accepted for service rendered.* | | |

The second entry is to take care of the accrual at the end of the period December 31, 2014.

**31-1=30days**

Therefore, the interest earned up to the 31$^{st}$ of December would be:

3,000 x 10% x 30/360 =25

### Journal

| Date | Account titles and explanation | Debit | Credit |
|---|---|---|---|
| 12/31/2014 | Interest receivable | 25 | |
| | Interest Revenue | | 25 |
| | *To record accrued interest earned on note.* | | |

When the note matures on March 1, 2015, Premier will make the following entry:

### Journal

| Date | Account titles and explanation | Debit | Credit |
|---|---|---|---|
| 03/01/2015 | Cash | 3,075 | |
| | Interest Revenue | | 50 |
| | Interest Receivable | | 25 |
| | Notes receivable | | 3,000 |

*To record the collection of note with interest earned.*

Interest revenue calculation

3000 x 10% x 60/360 = 50

## Recognizing Long Term Notes Receivable

Within this section, we need to examine if the value of the cash/ service/goods given up is equal to the cash received to determine whether the issuance of a note is at face value, interest bearing or zero interest. We are using the time value of money rate to assist us in making the calculation.

Let us start by highlighting the fact that the creation of these notes is from cash loans granted by companies to others or the value of goods/ services provided on a long term basis with the expectation of receiving money.

The fact that we have mentioned earlier that all notes do have an interest component to them, we now have to pay careful attention to how the interest rates affect these long-term notes.

It is important to point out that the value of the cash or goods exchanged is equal to the present value of the note to be received.

These recorded values are dependent on the issuance of the note at face value or not at face value. The note issued at face value means that the cash paid out or the value of the goods given up on day one is equal to the cash collection on the maturity date. Therefore, particular attention must be paid to the stated interest rate versus the market (yield) rate.

If the issuance of a note is not at face value, then it is issued either as an interest bearing note or a zero-interest bearing note. The collection of interest on these long-term notes is in accordance with the agreed period.

**Note issued at face value**

There are times when the value of the cash exchanged is equal to the value of the note to be received; this is when the issued note is at *face value*. The note issued at face value means that the cash paid out or the value of the goods issued on day one is equal to the cash collection on the maturity date. This issuance means that the state interest rate and the market interest rate are the same. (Stated interest rate = Market interest rate).

## Illustration XXX

In simpler terms, Premier Business Services granted a loan to JOAH Trading on 12/31/2012, and received a note for $12,000 at an annual interest rate of 8% for three years. If the market rate of similar risk is also 8% annually, it means that the cash Premier handed over to JOAH also equals to $12,000.

Note that, the present value of this 3-year note is also equal to $12,000 because the stated interest rate of 8% is equal to the current market rate of 8%.

To show the calculation of the proceeds to hand over to JOAH Company we find the present value of the note by making the following computation:

Face value of the note (Principal amount) $12,000
Present value of the principal amount:
(This is the amount $12,000 in three years' time
equals to presently)

*Note that, the market rate is used to determine the present value but remember that the stated rate and the market rate are the same under this scenario. Therefore, the usage of any of the rates for the calculation is okay.*

The time value of money rate for 3 periods @ 8% is 0.79383 for a single sum: (See table below).
$12,000 (PVF 3, 8%) =$12,000 x 0.79383        9,525.96
Present value of the interest amount to be collected:
(This is what the annual receipt of $960
for three periods will be equal to at present)
The time value of money rate for an annuity
amount for 3 periods @ 8% is 2.57710:
(See table below)
960 (PVF-OA 3, 8%) = 960 X 2.57710        2,474.04
                                                                    12,000
Difference                                                          0

*Note that, since the difference in amount is zero, then there is nothing to amortize.*

## Table showing present value of 1 or a single sum

| 8% | 9% | 10% | 11% | 12% | 15% | (n) Periods |
|---|---|---|---|---|---|---|
| .92593 | .91743 | .90909 | .90090 | .89286 | .86957 | 1 |
| .85734 | .84168 | .82645 | .81162 | .79719 | .75614 | 2 |
| .79383 | .77218 | .75132 | .73119 | .71178 | .65752 | 3 |
| .73503 | .70843 | .68301 | .65873 | .63552 | .57175 | 4 |
| .68058 | .64993 | .62092 | .59345 | .56743 | .49718 | 5 |
| .63017 | .59627 | .56447 | .53464 | .50663 | .43233 | 6 |
| .58349 | .54703 | .51316 | .48166 | .45235 | .37594 | 7 |
| .54027 | .50187 | .46651 | .43393 | .40388 | .32690 | 8 |
| .50025 | .46043 | .42410 | .39092 | .36061 | .28426 | 9 |
| .46319 | .42241 | .38554 | .35218 | .32197 | .24719 | 10 |

## Table showing present value of an ordinary annuity of 1

| 8% | 9% | 10% | 11% | 12% | 15% | (n) Periods |
|---|---|---|---|---|---|---|
| .92593 | .91743 | .90909 | .90090 | .89286 | .86957 | 1 |
| 1.78326 | 1.75911 | 1.73554 | 1.71252 | 1.69005 | 1.62571 | 2 |
| 2.57710 | 2.53130 | 2.48685 | 2.44371 | 2.40183 | 2.28323 | 3 |
| 3.31213 | 3.23972 | 3.16986 | 3.10245 | 3.03735 | 2.85498 | 4 |
| 3.99271 | 3.88965 | 3.79079 | 3.69590 | 3.60478 | 3.35216 | 5 |
| 4.62288 | 4.48592 | 4.35526 | 4.23054 | 4.11141 | 3.78448 | 6 |
| 5.20637 | 5.03295 | 4.86842 | 4.71220 | 4.56376 | 4.16042 | 7 |
| 5.74664 | 5.53482 | 5.33493 | 5.14612 | 4.96764 | 4.48732 | 8 |
| 6.24689 | 5.99525 | 5.75902 | 5.53705 | 5.32825 | 4.77158 | 9 |
| 6.71008 | 6.41766 | 6.14457 | 5.88923 | 5.65022 | 5.01877 | 10 |

The following shows you how Premier would record the journal entries:

### Journal

| Date | Account titles and explanation | Debit | Credit |
|---|---|---|---|
| 12/31/2012 | Notes receivable | 12,000 | |
| | Cash | | 12,000 |

*To record the note issued at face value.*

*Premier will be recognizing interest earned for each of the three years as follows:*

*12000 x 8% = 960*

### Journal

| Date | Account titles and explanation | Debit | Credit |
|---|---|---|---|
| 12/31/2013 | Cash | 960 | |
| | Interest revenue | | 960 |
| | *To record interest earned on note.* | | |

### Journal

| Date | Account titles and explanation | Debit | Credit |
|---|---|---|---|
| 12/31/2014 | Cash | 960 | |
| | Interest revenue | | 960 |
| | *To record interest earned on note.* | | |

**Note that, at the final date of interest received (Maturity date); JOAH Trading also paid back the principal amount of $12,000.**

### Journal

| Date | Account titles and explanation | Debit | Credit |
|---|---|---|---|
| 12/31/2015 | Cash | 12,960 | |
| | Interest revenue | | 960 |
| | Notes receivable | | 12,000 |
| | *To record collection of note with interest earned.* | | |

### Notes that are not issued at face value

The most important aspect to observe is that any note not issued at face value is issued as an *Interest-bearing* (stated rate and market rate are not the same) or a *Zero-interest-bearing note.*

*Note: Market interest rate, yield rate and effective interest rate are the same.*

### Interest Bearing Note

Once a note is issued at a stated interest rate that is not equal to the market interest rate (stated interest rate =/= market interest rate or the effective interest rate) at the time of issuance of the note, we can conclude that the issuance of this note *is not* at face value.

This issuance means that there is a discount or a premium on the note.

**The following example examines the issuance of a note receivable at a discount.**

## Illustration XXX1

Let us look at a typical example where Premier Business Services granted a loan on 12/31/2012, to JOAH Trading and received a three-year note of $15,000 with a stated interest rate of 8%, while the market interest rate of similar note is 10%.

*Note that, the market rate is 10%.*

We begin our computation to determine the value of the note by examining the present value of the principal amount to be collected at maturity along with the present value of the expected interest collection.

This calculation tells us the amount of cash Premier paid over to JOAH on 12/31/2012. The stated interest rate of 8% is less than the market rate of 10% hence the note is at a discount and the cash paid out on day one to JOAH is less than $15,000.

| | |
|---|---:|
| Face value of the note | $15,000 |
| Present value of the principal amount: | |

*Note that, the market rate will be used in finding the present value of the note.*

| | |
|---|---:|
| 15,000 (PVF 3, 10%) = $15,000 X 0.75132 | 11,270 |
| (See table in previous example for rate) | |
| Present value of the interest amount to be collected: | |
| 1,200 (PVF-OA 3, 10%) = 1,200 X 2.48685 | 2,984 |
| (See table in previous example for rate) | |
| Present value of the note | 14,254 |
| Amount discounted on the note | 746 |

What this means, is that, Premier paid out $746 less in cash than the face value of the note while receiving interest calculated on the face value of the note for the three years, plus the return of the $15,000 (face value) at the end of the three years. There is an amortization of the $746 over a three-year period and added to revenue thus effectively increasing the yearly interest revenue earned on the note.

Journal entry to record the note receivable is as follows:

**Journal**

| Date | Account titles and explanation | Debit | Credit |
|---|---|---|---|
| 12/31/2012 | Notes receivable | 15,000 | |
| | Discount on notes receivable | | 746 |
| | Cash | | 14,254 |
| | To record the note issued at a discount. | | |

**Amortization schedule for discount on a note receivable**
**Straight line method**
Stated rate 8%, market rate 10%

| Date | Cash Received (15,000 X 8%) | Interest revenue | Discount Amortized | Carrying value of note |
|---|---|---|---|---|
| 12/31/2012 | | | | 14,254 |
| Dec. 31, 2013 | 1,200 | 1,449*** | 249* | 14,503** |
| Dec. 31, 2014 | 1,200 | 1,449 | 249* | 14,752 |
| Dec. 31, 2015 | 1,200 | 1,448 | 248 | 15,000 |

*746/3 = 249(Rounded to the nearest dollar)
 249 + 249 + 248 (rounded) =746
**14,254 + 249 =14,503
***1,200 + 249 = 1,449

Note that, the straight line method is simply dividing the total discount by the term of the note.

## Journal
### (Repeated also in 2014)

| Date | Account titles and explanation | Debit | Credit |
|---|---|---|---|
| 12/31/2013 | Cash | 1,200 | |
| | Discount on notes receivable | 249 | |
| | Interest revenue | | 1,449 |
| | *To record interest earned on note.* | | |

**The journal entry at maturity is as follows:**

**Journal**

| Date | Account titles and explanation | Debit | Credit |
|---|---|---|---|
| 12/31/2015 | Cash | 16,200 | |
| | Discount on notes receivable | 248 | |
| | Interest revenue | | 1,448 |
| | Notes Receivable | | 15,000 |
| | *To record collection of note with interest earned.* | | |

Alternatively, the amortization of the interest can also be done by using another method of calculation which is the effective method. If you look carefully at the total discount amortized, you will see that both the straight line and the effective method have the same amount of discount amortized.

## Amortization schedule for discount on a note receivable
## Effective interest method
### Stated rate 8%, market rate 10%

| Date | Cash Received (15,000X8%) | Interest revenue (Carrying value X 10%) | Discount Amortized | Carrying value of note |
|---|---|---|---|---|
| 12/31/2012 | | | | 14,254 |
| 12/31/2013 | 1,200 | 1,425 | 225* | 14,479** |
| 12/31/2014 | 1,200 | 1,448 | 248 | 14,727 |
| 12/31/2015 | 1,200 | 1,473 | 273 | 15,000 |

*1425 - 1200 = 225
**14,254 + 225 = 14,479

Premier's journal entries to record interest revenue under the effective method are:

### Journal

| Date | Account titles and explanation | Debit | Credit |
|---|---|---|---|
| 12/31/2013 | Cash | 1,200 | |
| | Discount on notes receivable | 225 | |
| | Interest revenue | | 1,425 |
| | *To record interest earned on note.* | | |

### Journal

| Date | Account titles and explanation | Debit | Credit |
|---|---|---|---|
| 12/31/2014 | Cash | 1,200 | |
| | Discount on notes receivable | 248 | |
| | Interest revenue | | 1,448 |
| | *To record interest earned on note.* | | |

The journal entry at maturity is as follows:

### Journal

| Date | Account titles and explanation | Debit | Credit |
|---|---|---|---|
| 12/31/2015 | Cash | 16,200 | |
| | Discount on notes receivable | 273 | |
| | Interest revenue | | 1,473 |
| | Notes Receivable | | 15,000 |
| | *To record collection of note with interest earned.* | | |

We now examine a note receivable issued at a premium.

## Illustration XXX11

Let us look at a typical example where Premier Business Services granted a loan on 12/31/2012 to JOAH Trading and received a three-year note of $15,000 with a stated interest rate of 12% while the market interest rate of similar note is 10%.

We begin our computation to determine the value of the note by examining the present value of the principal amount along with the present value of the expected interest collection.

This calculation will tell us the amount of cash Premier will actually pay over to JOAH on 12/31/2012. The stated interest rate of 12% is more than the market rate of 10%, hence, the note is at a premium and the cash paid out on day one is more than $15,000.

Face value of the note $15,000
Present value of the principal amount:

**Note that, the market rate will be used in finding the present value of the note.**

| | | |
|---|---|---|
| 15,000 (PVF 3, 10%) = $15,000 X 0.75132 | 11,270 | |
| Present value of the interest amount to be collected: | | |
| 1,800 (PVF-OA 3, 10%) = 1,800 X 2.48685 | 4,476 | |
| Present value of the note | | 15,746 |
| Premium paid on note | | 746 |

What this means, is that, Premier paid out $746 more in cash than the face value of the note while receiving interest only on the face value for three years plus the return of the $15,000 (face value) at the end of the three years. There is an amortization of the $746 over a three-year period and added to expense thus effectively reducing the yearly interest revenue earned on the note.

### Journal entry

| Date | Account titles and explanation | Debit | Credit |
|---|---|---|---|
| 12/31/2012 | Notes receivable | 15,000 | |
| | Premium on notes receivable | 746 | |
| | Cash | | 15,746 |
| | To record the note issued at a premium. | | |

## Amortization schedule for premium on a note receivable
### Effective interest method
### Stated rate 12%, market rate 10%

| Date | Cash Received (15,000X12%) | Interest revenue (Carrying value X 10%) | Premium Amortized | Carrying value of note |
|---|---|---|---|---|
| 12/31/2012 | | | | 15,746 |
| 12/31/2013 | 1,800 | 1,575 | 225* | 15,521** |
| 12/31/2014 | 1,800 | 1,552 | 248 | 15,273 |
| 12/31/2015 | 1,800 | 1,527 | 273 | 15,000 |

*1800 − 1575 = 225
**15,746 - 225 = 15,521

### Journal

| Date | Account titles and explanation | Debit | Credit |
|---|---|---|---|
| 12/31/2013 | Cash | 1,800 | |
| | Premium on notes receivable | | 225 |
| | Interest revenue | | 1,575 |
| | *To record interest earned on note.* | | |

### Journal

| Date | Account titles and explanation | Debit | Credit |
|---|---|---|---|
| 12/31/2014 | Cash | 1,800 | |
| | Premium on notes receivable | | 248 |
| | Interest revenue | | 1,552 |
| | *To record interest earned on note.* | | |

The journal entry at maturity is as follows:

### Journal

| Date | Account titles and explanation | Debit | Credit |
|---|---|---|---|
| 12/31/2015 | Cash | 16,800 | |
| | Premium on notes receivable | | 273 |
| | Interest revenue | | 1,527 |
| | Notes Receivable | | 15,000 |
| | *To record collection of note with interest earned.* | | |

## Zero- Interest Bearing Note

This scenario is when there is an assignment of a zero interest rate to a note, and the receipt of the cash by the issuer of the note is being used to determine the present value of the note. The repayment amount at the maturity (future) date less the amount of cash initially received equates to the discount on the note. The rate that is used to determine the difference between the amount of cash received and the repayment is called the implicit rate.

## Illustration XXX111

Premier Business Services received a note on December 31, 2012, from JOAH Trading of $20,000 in return for cash granted of $16,439. The note is Zero-Interest bearing and matures in five years.

Based on the cash received by JOAH of $16,439 which is the present value and the amount of $20,000 (future value) to be repaid to Premier in five years, the implicit rate would be equal to approx. 4%.

| | | |
|---|---|---|
| Amount to be received by Premier at maturity date 12/31/2017 | | $20,000 |
| Amount paid out by Premier to JOAH on 12/31/2012 | | 16,439 |
| Discount on the note | | 3,561 |

What this means, is that, Premier paid out $3,561 less in cash than the face value of the note. There is an amortization of this amount over a five-year period and added to revenue yearly.

The Journal entry to record this transaction is:

### Journal

| Date | Account titles and Explanation | Debit | Credit |
|---|---|---|---|
| 12/31/2012 | Notes receivable | 20,000 | |
| | Discount on notes receivable | | 3,561 |
| | Cash | | 16,439 |

*To record issuance of zero interest bearing note.*

### Amortization schedule for discount on a note receivable
### Effective interest method
### 0% note, discounted at 4%

| Date | Cash Received (15,000X0%) | Interest revenue (Carrying value X 4%) | Discount Amortized | Carrying value of note |
|---|---|---|---|---|
| 12/31/2012 | | | | 16,439 |
| 12/31/2013 | 0 | 658 | 658 | 17,097 |
| 12/31/2014 | 0 | 684 | 684 | 17,781 |
| 12/31/2015 | 0 | 711 | 711 | 18,492 |
| 12/31/2016 | 0 | 740 | 740 | 19,232 |
| 12/31/2017 | 0 | 768 | 768* | 20,000 |
| | | | 3,561 | |

*769 is rounded down to 768

The interest revenue as a journal entry for Premier at the end of the **first period** is as follows:

### Journal entry

| Date | Account titles and explanation | Debit | Credit |
|---|---|---|---|
| 12/31/2013 | Discount on notes receivable | 658 | |
| | Interest revenue | | 658 |
| | *To record interest earned on note.* | | |

The journal entry at maturity is as follows:

### Journal

| Date | Account titles and explanation | Debit | Credit |
|---|---|---|---|
| 12/31/2017 | Cash | 20,000 | |
| | Discount on notes receivable | 768 | |
| | Interest revenue | | 768 |
| | Notes Receivable | | 20,000 |
| | *To record collection of note with interest earned.* | | |

# Valuation of Notes Receivable

Based on a ruling of the FASB, companies now have the option to record some of their assets at fair value as opposed to historical cost. We provide you with an understanding of the two components:

The *fair value* of an asset is the price that one would currently receive from the sale of that asset in a normal market setting on a particular date. In the context of a note receivable, there are times when the value of the receivable changes based on time, when compared to the original value. That is, the current value may not be equal to the original value because of impairment.

Impairment is the result that causes the company not to be able to collect all of the receivables outstanding. This impairment can cause from either bankruptcy declaration of the customer or an expressed difficulty in meeting payments.

Example: On January 01, 2015, Premier Business Services received a note for $500,000 but on December 31, 2015, they realized that due to some impairment the current value of the note is $480,000.

*Historical cost,* on the other hand, reflects the price paid for the asset on the original date of the transaction. Supporters of this method argue that it is far more reliable and verifiable than fair value since the fair value can be more biased.

In determining the value of a note receivable, we must first draw the distinction between that of a short-term note and a long-term note.

## Short-Term Notes

The method of valuing short-term notes receivable can be easily compared to that of accounts receivable since the methodology is the same regarding the determination of the uncollectible amount.

## Illustration XXX1V

| | |
|---|---:|
| Notes receivable | 200,000 |
| Uncollectible amount | (5,000) |
| Net amount | 195,000 |

## Long-Term Notes

These on the other hand, are examined differently regarding the method used to arrive at a valuation amount. Companies can choose to adopt the fair value approach or the historical cost approach in determining the value of the notes receivable they report on their financial statements. One important thing to note is that irrespective of the method a company chooses to use in recognizing the value of a receivable, it must maintain the utilization of that method for the receivable in question until it relinquishes that particular receivable.

Even though the usage of the fair value approach is one method of determining the value of the receivable which of course is an asset, companies have to remain mindful of the **cost principle** of accounting if the value of this asset increases. That is, there should be no recording of the increase of this asset value on the balance sheet.

Alternatively, if the receivable lost or suffered impairment in value, based on the constraint of *conservatism,* a company can record the decrease in value on the balance sheet and carry the loss on the income statement.

## Illustration XXXV

### Balance Sheet

| | |
|---|---|
| Notes Receivable | $500,000 |
| Impairment loss | (20,000) |
| Net Receivables | 480,000 |

### Income Statement

Other Gains or Losses

| | |
|---|---|
| Impairment loss on receivables | 20,000 |

# Disposition (Selling) of Accounts Receivable

There are times when a company wants to hasten the collection of the cash outstanding, and the reasons can be many. Two of the main ones include the need for improvement in cash flow and the relieving of itself from the collection effort. A quick way to improve the cash flow position is achieved by the selling of the accounts receivable or pledging them as security for loans.

Let us examine these two efforts.

## The Selling of Accounts Receivable (Factoring)

The company usually makes the sale of the receivables to a bank or a finance company that is called a *Factor*. This factor purchases the receivables from the company for a factoring fee and then handles all the collections involved. The company in return gets access to the cash earlier and saves itself from the hassle of the collection process. Note that, this is *not* a loan to the Factor but basically, the Factor assuming the debt.

While this might sound good at the outset, companies have the challenge of proving the creditworthiness of their customers to the factor so as to get the best rate charged because the credit rating of the customers is more important than that of the company to the factor.

The factor charges a fee at most times of 5% or more of the receivables that the company sold to them. In addition to the fee charged, the Factoring Company withhold an amount to cover amounts that are uncollectibles, sales discounts or sales returns and allowances. After the company and the factor reach an agreement on the terms and conditions of the sale, a "Notice of Assignment" is then sent to the customers informing them to make payments now to the factor. A "lock box" is established to facilitate the payments from the customers and the factor can then receive payments.

With the factoring transaction, a company has the option of selling the receivables either *with recourse* or *without recourse.*

## With recourse

A sale of the receivables to the factor *with recourse* is an agreement that total risk of the collection is not passed on to the buyer. What this means is that, if the factor cannot collect on these accounts, the company that makes the sale is liable to the factor for any uncollectible amount. An amount is withheld by the factor to cover any uncollectibles, sales discounts or sales returns and allowances. As a result of this arrangement, the seller has to establish a liability referred to as a *recourse liability* at the time of the sales transaction to take care of the uncollectibles.

## Illustration XXXV1

Let us assume that Premier Business Services sold $200,000 worth of receivables to a Finance Company that gave a cash advance of $180,000 and retained $14,000 to take care of any adjustments such as uncollectible accounts, sales discounts or sales returns and allowances. The Finance Company charges a factoring fee of $6,000. Based on experience, it has been determined that the Finance Company may not collect approximately $5,000, and since there is a need to observe the rule of conservatism, this amount needs to be captured as part of the loss. Therefore, the total accounts receivable is 200,000 (180,000 + 14,000 + 6,000) and the loss on sale is $11,000 ($6,000 + $5,000).

The **journal entry** to record this is as follows:

| Date | Account titles and explanation | Debit | Credit |
|---|---|---|---|
| 12/20/2014 | Cash | 180,000 | |
| | Due from Factor | 14,000 | |
| | Loss on sale of receivables | 11,000 | |
| |     Receivables | | 200,000 |
| |     Recourse liability | | 5,000 |
| | *To record the sale of accounts receivable and recourse liability.* | | |

In the event that the Factor is able to collect the entire $200,000 the **journal entry** will be as follows:

| Date | Account titles and explanation | Debit | Credit |
|---|---|---|---|
| 03/01/2015 | Cash | 14,000 | |
| | Recourse liability | 5,000 | |
| |     Gain on sale of receivable | | 5,000 |
| |     Due from factor | | 14,000 |
| | *To record the full amount due from factor.* | | |

If the Factor is only able to collect $198,000, it will remit to Premier, an additional $12,000 (18,000 − 6,000). Then the transaction will be posted to the **journal** as follows:

| Date | Account titles and explanation | Debit | Credit |
|---|---|---|---|
| 03/01/2015 | Cash | 12,000 | |
| | Recourse liability | 5,000 | |
| | Gain on sale from receivable | | 3,000 |
| | Due from factor | | 14,000 |
| | To record a partial amount received as due from factor. | | |

Note that effectively, the total loss would now be 6,000 + 2,000 = 8,000
Fee of $6,000 + (200,000 − 198,000)

Should the Factor only collect their advance payment plus fee of $186,000 (180,000 + 6,000) and the additional $14,000 is deemed uncollectible, the journal entry would be:

| Date | Account title and Explanation | Debit | Credit |
|---|---|---|---|
| 03/01/15 | Loss on sale of receivable | 9,000 | |
| | Recourse liability | 5,000 | |
| | Due from factor | | 14,000 |
| | To record zero amounts received as due from factor. | | |

Note that, total loss on sale of receivable 200,000
−180,000
20,000 (6,000 + 5,000 + 9,000)

Note that under this arrangement, the factoring company will not experience any bad debts from uncollectibles.

## Without recourse

This type of sale occurs when the Factoring Company takes full responsibility for the risk involved in the collection process. That is, the Factor absorb any loss incurred (uncollectible) with the collection of the accounts but withholds a portion of the funds referred to as *amount due from factor* to cover any possible sales returns, discounts or allowances. Whenever a Factoring Company purchases receivables without recourse, they charge a higher factoring fee because of the additional risk involved.

Under this type of arrangement, the entries in the journal are much simpler.

Let us examine the same example, but this time, the sale of the receivables is without recourse.

## Illustration XXXV11

The facts of the argument are the same as in the previous example where Premier sold $200,000 worth of receivables to a Bank and received $180,000 as an advance payment. Since the sale of these receivables is without recourse, a fee of $10,000 is charged by the Bank because the risk increases. A point to note is that there is no estimation of liability, and the Bank retains $10,000 for any adjustments of discounts, returns or allowances.

The **journal entry** to accommodate this transaction is:

| Date | Accounts titles and explanation | Debit | Credit |
|---|---|---|---|
| 12/20/2014 | Cash | 180,000 | |
| | Due from factor | 10,000 | |
| | Loss on sale of receivable | 10,000 | |
| | Receivables | | 200,000 |

*To record the sale of accounts receivable.*

If the factor collects the full amount and pays you the retainer of $10,000, you will do the following journal entry:

| Date | Account titles and explanation | Debit | Credit |
|---|---|---|---|
| 03/01/2015 | Cash | 10,000 | |
| | Due from factor | | 10,000 |
| | *To record the receipt of amount due from factor.* | | |

If after the collection process the Factor can only pay over an additional $8,000 to Premier, because the customers have taken allowances of $2,000, then the entry would be:

| Date | Account titles and explanation | Debit | Credit |
|---|---|---|---|
| 03/01/2015 | Cash | 8,000 | |
| | Sales allowance | 2,000 | |
| | Due from factor | | 10,000 |
| | *To record the receipt of amount due from factor less allowance.* | | |

**Note that under this type of arrangement, the factoring company is likely to experience some bad debts which will result from uncollectibles.**

## Bridging the gap

At the time of writing, there is a company that currently acts as a go-between seller and buyer especially for cross-border trade, their system connects to the purchaser, and that provides the seller with a signal as to when there is an approval of the invoice. The seller can then sell the approved invoice to a financial institution and receives cash before the due date of the invoice.

# Pledging of receivables

The pledging of the receivables is another way companies can improve their cash flow position by borrowing money and using their receivables as security for the loan. This type of transaction *does not* shift the risk of collection from the company (borrower) because the title of ownership remains with the borrower. Therefore, if the company fails to repay the loan, the Bank can insist that the company uses the remaining collection of receivables to offset any loan amount outstanding.

## Illustration XXXVlll

On January 01, 2015, Premier Business Services pledged $150,000 of its receivables as collateral for a 90-day note of $100,000 from a Bank. The bank charged a 0.8% financing fee and interest rate of 10% on the loan.

Premier would make a note on its financial statement to show that the receivable amount of $150,000 was pledged to secure a note payable of $100,000.

Let's look at Premier's journal entry to record this transaction:

| Date | Account titles and explanation | Debit | Credit |
|---|---|---|---|
| 01/01/2015 | Cash | 99,200 | |
| | Financing fee | 800 | |
| | (100,000 x 0.8%) | | |
| | Notes Payable | | 100,000 |

If Premier makes a collection of $52,000 from the accounts receivable for the month of January, after recording the necessary receipt of the cash by debiting cash and crediting receivables, it can make the following allocation towards the payment of the loan.

| Date | Account titles and explanation | Debit | Credit |
|---|---|---|---|
| 02/01/2015 | Interest expense | 833 | |
| | (100,000x10%x30/360) | | |
| | Notes payable | 51,167 | |
| | Cash | | 52,000 |

The collection of accounts receivable for the remaining months of the note would be applied to the loan until it is entirely paid off.

# Some important Ratios

**Accounts receivable ratio** is used as one of the primary measurements in analyzing the quality and liquidity of the receivables. It tells you the rate at which the company is collecting its receivables. The numerator is preferably net credit sales, and the denominator is the average between the beginning and ending net accounts or trade receivable balance.

The formula is:

$$\text{Accounts Receivable Turnover} = \frac{\text{Net Sales}}{\text{Average accounts or trade receivable (net)}}$$

## Illustration XXX1X

If Premier Business Services reported net credit sales of $975,000, beginning and ending of period accounts receivable are $180,000 and $140,000 respectively. Calculate the rate of turnover for the accounts receivable.

$$= \frac{975,000}{(180,000 + 140,000)/2}$$

$$= \frac{975,000}{160,000}$$

$$= 6 \text{ times}$$

**The average collection period is** 365/6 = 61 days.

This collection period means that Premier converts its accounts receivable balance into cash six times throughout the one-year period, or it takes an average of 61 days to collect its accounts receivable.

# Rent receivable

This account is used to record rent earned but not yet collected. Most times if the tenant is required to pay their rent on a particular due date but remains unpaid after the due date, then there would be rent owed by the tenant. The rent owed by the tenant is *rent receivable which is a current asset.*

## Illustration XL

Premier Business Services is the Landlord, and Tenant Z is required to pay his/her rent of $4,000 on December 01, 2015. If the rent is outstanding on December 31, 2015, at the closure of the books, then the amount owed by Tenant Z is recorded as rent receivable and also rent revenue earned.

See the journal entry below:

**Journal**

| Date | Account titles and explanation | Debit | Credit |
|---|---|---|---|
| 12/31/2015 | Rent receivable | 4,000 | |
| | Rent revenue | | 4,000 |
| | *To record outstanding rent for December.* | | |

# Lease Receivable

Lease arrangement is a very popular type of commercial transaction that involves passing the permitted use of an asset from one party to the next. That is, the person receiving the asset to use is the lessee and the person (the owner) giving up the asset is the lessor. This type of transaction is a contractual arrangement where the lessee agrees to pay the lessor for the use of the asset for a specified amount of time. With lease transactions, many different types or scenarios involve the lessor and the lessee.

Since we are looking at the **receivable** side of the business for this book, our focus only includes the lessor. We will examine how to handle accounting transactions as they relate to the money owed.

We now apply the argument regarding a company who is acting as the lessee versus another that is acting as the lessor. Whenever a lessor's company enters into a lease transaction, there are at least three types of contractual arrangements that are likely to form. They are operating lease, direct financing, and sales-type lease.

**Operating lease**

Firstly, with operating lease, the payments collected by the lessor are referred to as rent. That is periodic rent is collected. If there is outstanding rent at the end of the accounting period, then rent receivable is set up.

## Illustration XL1

Let's assume that Premier Business Services is the lessor and Company Z leased a computer and paid a monthly rental of $210 on the first of each month. If December's rent is outstanding at the time of closing the books on December 31, 2015, then the adjusting entry would be recorded as follows.

Note: This rent would have been due on December 1, 2015, but unpaid at the time of closing the books on December 31, 2015.

See the journal entry below for Premier Business Services:

### Journal

| Date | Account titles and explanation | Debit | Credit |
|---|---|---|---|
| 12/31/2015 | Rent receivable | 210 | |
| | Rent revenue | | 210 |
| | To record outstanding rent for December. | | |

## Direct financing

Another area that the issue of lease receivable appears in transactions relating to leases is under the heading of direct financing. While in this scenario the lessor also hands over the asset to the lessee, an important point to note is that the lessor gives up the right to the lessee to take depreciation expense of the asset, and therefore, only looks forward to collecting the lease payments.

The lessor then records the cost of the asset as a receivable on the books while the collection of the lease payments represents an amortized portion of the receivable along with the interest revenue.

The following example allows you to appreciate the various steps involved in the calculation and how to record the transactions.

## Illustration XL11

Premier Business Services leased a piece of equipment on 01/01/2013, to JOAH Trading with an annual lease payment of $14,340 payable on January 1$^{st}$ each year. The cost of the equipment is $50,000 and the term of the lease four years. The life of the asset is also four years with **no residual value.**

Premier uses a rate of 10%.

**Premier Business Services – Lessor's book**

| Date | Annual lease receipt | 10% interest | Reduction of lease receivable | Lease receivable (Principal amount) |
|---|---|---|---|---|
| 01/01/2013 | | | | 50,000 |
| 01/01/2013 | 14,340 | -0- | 14,340 | 35,660 |
| 01/01/2014 | 14,340 | 3,566* | 10,774** | 24,886 |
| 01/01/2015 | 14,340 | 2,489 | 11,851 | 13,035 |
| 01/01/2016 | 14,340 | 1,305 | 13,035 | ----0---- |

*35,660 X 10% = 3,566
**14,340 – 3566 = 10,774

## Journal

| Date | Account titles and explanation | Debit | Credit |
|---|---|---|---|
| 01/01/2013 | Lease receivable | 50,000 | |
| | Equipment | | 50,000 |
| | To record the lease of the equipment. | | |

## Journal

| Date | Account titles and explanation | Debit | Credit |
|---|---|---|---|
| 01/01/2013 | Cash | 14,340 | |
| | Lease receivable | | 14,340 |
| | To record the first lease payment. | | |

## Journal

| Date | Account titles and explanation | Debit | Credit |
|---|---|---|---|
| 12/31/2013 | Interest receivable | 3,566 | |
| | Interest revenue | | 3,566 |
| | To record the accrued interest at year end. | | |

## Journal

| Date | Account titles and explanation | Debit | Credit |
|---|---|---|---|
| 01/01/2014 | Cash | 14,340 | |
| | Lease receivable | | 10,774 |
| | Interest receivable | | 3,566 |
| | To record the collection of lease payment. | | |

Note: The $10,774 reduced the lease receivable (principal amount), while the $3,566 represented interest.

**Journal**

| Date | Account titles and explanation | Debit | Credit |
|---|---|---|---|
| 12/31/2014 | Interest receivable | 2,489 | |
| | Interest revenue | | 2,489 |
| | *To record the accrued interest at year end.* | | |

**Journal**

| Date | Account titles and explanation | Debit | Credit |
|---|---|---|---|
| 01/01/2015 | Cash | 14,340 | |
| | Lease receivable | | 11,851 |
| | Interest receivable | | 2,489 |
| | *To record the collection of lease payment.* | | |

**Journal**

| Date | Account titles and explanation | Debit | Credit |
|---|---|---|---|
| 12/31/2015 | Interest receivable | 1,305 | |
| | Interest revenue | | 1,305 |
| | *To record the accrued interest at year end.* | | |

**Journal**

| Date | Account titles and explanation | Debit | Credit |
|---|---|---|---|
| 01/01/2016 | Cash | 14,340 | |
| | Lease receivable | | 13,035 |
| | Interest receivable | | 1,305 |
| | *To record the collection of lease payment.* | | |

## Sales-type lease

This transaction is another type of lease arrangement where you see the issue of receivables being a part of the transaction. The accounting treatment is the same as in direct financing; the only difference is that gross profit is recognized at the start of the lease period because the transaction might involve **a manufacturer who is also acting as the lessor. (Continuing with the previous example)** Please note that the present value of the total lease payments (14,340 x four-year annuity due factor of 3.48685) would equal the selling price of the item $50,000 and the subtraction of a cost of goods sold $38,000 would allow us to have an immediate gross profit of $12,000. Since we are collecting the selling price in four payments, there is an interest component which forms part of the lease payments. We recognize this interest over the duration of the lease as in the direct financing.

## Illustration XL111

Looking at the previous example above with the same amortization schedule and applying a Sales Type Lease arrangement, we would set up the initial transaction similar to making a sale of inventory items.

**The journal entries would be as follow:**

### Journal

| Date | Account titles and explanation | Debit | Credit |
|---|---|---|---|
| 01/01/2013 | Lease receivable | 50,000 | |
| | Sales revenue | | 50,000 |
| | Cost of goods sold | 38,000 | |
| | Inventory | | 38,000 |
| | *To record the lease of the equipment.* | | |

### Journal

| Date | Account titles and explanation | Debit | Credit |
|---|---|---|---|
| 01/01/2013 | Cash | 14,340 | |
| | Lease receivable | | 14,340 |
| | *To record the first lease payment.* | | |

### Journal

| Date | Account titles and explanation | Debit | Credit |
|---|---|---|---|
| 12/31/2013 | Interest receivable | 3,566 | |
| | Interest revenue | | 3,566 |
| | *To record the accrued interest at year end.* | | |

### Journal

| Date | Account titles and explanation | Debit | Credit |
|---|---|---|---|
| 01/01/2014 | Cash | 14,340 | |
| | Lease receivable | | 10,774 |
| | Interest receivable | | 3,566 |
| | *To record the collection of lease payment.* | | |

*Note: The $10,774 reduced the lease receivable (principal amount), while the $3,566 represented interest.*

## Journal

| Date | Account titles and explanation | Debit | Credit |
|---|---|---|---|
| 12/31/2014 | Interest receivable | 2,489 | |
| | Interest revenue | | 2,489 |

*To record the accrued interest at year end.*

## Journal

| Date | Account titles and explanation | Debit | Credit |
|---|---|---|---|
| 01/01/2015 | Cash | 14,340 | |
| | Lease receivable | | 11,851 |
| | Interest receivable | | 2,489 |

*To record the collection of lease payment.*

## Journal

| Date | Account titles and explanation | Debit | Credit |
|---|---|---|---|
| 12/31/2015 | Interest receivable | 1,305 | |
| | Interest revenue | | 1,305 |

*To record the accrued interest at year end.*

## Journal

| Date | Account titles and explanation | Debit | Credit |
|---|---|---|---|
| 01/01/2016 | Cash | 14,340 | |
| | Lease receivable | | 13,035 |
| | Interest receivable | | 1,305 |

*To record the collection of lease payment.*

# Interest receivable

There are instances when the interest earned is recorded on the books as revenue even though the company or bank granting the loan has not yet made any interest collection.

## Illustration XLIV

If Premier Business Services received a 8% note of $10,000 for 90 days from customer Z on December 01, 2015, and Premier is closing its books on December 31, 2015. They make a calculation of 8% x 10,000 x 30/360 = 66.67 to determine the interest revenue earned for the period December 01-31 (30 days).

See the journal entry below:

| Date | Accounts titles and explanation | Debit | Credit |
|---|---|---|---|
| 12/31/2015 | Interest receivable | 66.67 | |
| | Interest revenue | | 66.67 |

# Dividends Receivable

Whenever your company owns stocks in any other company, and that company declares a dividend; at the date of declaration and before the payment is made, your company can therefore record this as dividends receivable.

**Illustration XLV**

Premier Business Services owns stocks in Corporation Z, and that Corporation has declared dividends on December 15, 2014, payable January 20, 2015. If the closure of Premier's books is on December 31, 2014, and Premier has not received the dividends as yet, then this can be recorded by Premier as dividends revenue and dividends receivable as a current asset.

If the dividend amount were, for example, $2,800, Premier would make the following journal entries:

| Date | Account title and explanation | Debit | Credit |
|---|---|---|---|
| 12/31/2014 | Dividends receivable | 2,800 | |
| | Dividends revenue | | 2,800 |
| | *To record dividends receivable.* | | |
| | | | |
| 01/20/2015 | Cash | 2,800 | |
| | Dividends receivable | | 2,800 |
| | *To record the cash collection.* | | |

# Cash advances to employees

Companies from time to time make cash advance payments to their employees. Many times this is done with the intention to recollect within a very short period. Whenever a company makes a cash advance, a debit is recorded to Advance to Employees Account and a credit to Cash Account. The company is likely to establish a system to withhold periodic payments from the employee's salary or wages. The recollection of this money has a debit recorded to Cash and a credit to Advance to Employees Account.

## Illustration XLV1

Let us look at an example of how to treat this type of transaction:

Premier Business Services made advance cash payments totaling $2,400 to their employees which are to be repaid equally over a six-month period.

The journal entry to record the advance payment is:

| Date | Account title and explanation | Debit | Credit |
|---|---|---|---|
| 01/01/2015 | Advance to employees | 2,400 | |
| | Cash | | 2,400 |
| | *To record cash advance to employees.* | | |

The journal entry to record the first monthly receipt of payment is:

| | | |
|---|---|---|
| 01/31/2015 | Cash | 400 |
| | Advance to employees | 400 |

*To record cash collection from employees.*

**Note that, the remaining five journal entries would be the same to reflect total collection.**

# Income Tax Receivable

This receivable is money that a company expects to receive as a refund from tax agencies such as the IRS, State or Municipal Tax Authorities. If a company paid more money to a tax agency for a particular period than what they should pay, then the excess would have been a receivable or a refund to the company. We might ask ourselves the question of how a situation like this could occur. The simple answer is that, there are instances when a company made estimated tax payments for a particular period before the completion of the tax return. If the estimated payments made are more than the actual amount owed, then the difference in amount represents an income tax receivable (income tax refund) to the company.

## Illustration XLV11

If during the year 2015, Premier Business Services made quarterly payments to the relevant tax authority totaling $325,000 but at the end of Premier's fiscal year, they realize that their 2015 tax obligation is $300,000. Premier Business Services would now record a receivable of $25,000 which would be the result of 325,000-300,000.

The journal entries to record these transactions would be:

*Note that, for the payments:*

| Date | Account titles and explanation | Debit | Credit |
|---|---|---|---|
| 03/31/2015 | Income tax expense | 81,250 | |
| | Cash | | 81,250 |
| | *To record estimated quarterly income tax expense.* | | |

| | | | |
|---|---|---|---|
| 06/30/2015 | Income tax expense | 81,250 | |
| | Cash | | 81,250 |
| | *To record estimated quarterly income tax expense.* | | |
| | | | |
| 09/30/2015 | Income tax expense | 81,250 | |
| | Cash | | 81,250 |
| | *To record estimated quarterly income tax expense.* | | |
| | | | |
| 12/31/2015 | Income tax expense | 81,250 | |
| | Cash | | 81,250 |
| | *To record estimated quarterly income tax expense.* | | |

Note that, for the receivable:

| Date | Account titles and explanation | Debit | Credit |
|---|---|---|---|
| 01/31/2016 | Accounts Receivable | 25,000 | |
| | Income tax expense | | 25,000 |
| | *To record excess income taxes paid as receivable.* | | |

Another situation of a company having to deal with income tax receivable is when they experience a net operating loss, and there is a loss carryback. We do not want to get into an extensive example regarding this type of transaction, and hence our effort to explain it is in a very simple format.

## Illustration XLV111

Let us consider, Premier Business Services made a profit in 2013 and 2014 of $78,000 and $55,300 respectively. However, for some unknown reason, they experienced a loss in 2015 of $147,000. Let's assume that an income tax rate of 35% is in effect.

Based on the law, the management of Premier has the option of applying the loss as a carryback up to two years in the past. What this means is that, since in 2015 they had a loss of $147,000 and there was profit each for 2013 and 2014. They can go back two years to recover the money paid as taxes for those years once it is below or equal to the current year's loss.

The taxes paid for 2013 and 2014 would be $27,300 (78,000x35%) and $19,355 (55,300x35%), therefore, the operating loss of $147,000 is greater than the taxable income totaling $133,300 (78,000+55,300) for the two previous years. The remaining loss of $13,700 (147,000-133,300) would be a carry forward.

The tax benefit as a result of the carryback would be $46,655 (27,300+19,355) is recognized as income tax refund receivable for 2015.

The journal entry to record this part of the transaction is:

| Date | Account titles and explanation | Debit | Credit |
|---|---|---|---|
| 01/01/2016 | Income tax refund receivable | 46,655 | |
| | Benefit due to loss carryback | | 46,655 |

*To record income tax refund receivable due to carryback.*

# Insurance Claims Receivable

There are times when a company might have experienced a loss or damage of property, and files an insurance claim with the respective insurance company. The injured company at their end would record a debit to Loss from Property Damage Account and a credit to the relevant Property Account that suffered the loss. Upon agreeing or signing any document for an amount of claim settlement, the injured company would record a debit to Insurance Claims Receivable and a credit to Loss from Property Damage Account.

**Note that, if a debit balance remained in the Loss from Property Damage Account; then that amount would have represented the actual loss from the property damage. However, if there is a credit balance, then there would have been a gain on the account from the property damage.**

## Illustration XL1X

Assume that Premier Business Services has a pending fire claim settlement to which it expects and already signed some form of commitment documents to receive from an insurance company the sum of $28,500. If Premier had previously adjusted a building account of $32,210 based on the damage and created a Loss from Property Damage Account with the same amount, then the journal entries would be as follow.

## Journal entries for the official estimate of the fire:

| Date | Account title and explanation | Debit | Credit |
|---|---|---|---|
| 03/10/1015 | Loss from Property Damage | 32,210 | |
| | Building | | 32,210 |
| | *To record Journal entry for the pending claim settlement.* | | |

| Date | Account title and explanation | Debit | Credit |
|---|---|---|---|
| 05/05/2015 | Insurance claim receivable | 28,500 | |
| | Loss from Property Damage | | 28,500 |
| | *To record proposed insurance settlement.* | | |

Debit   32,210
Credit  <u>28,500</u>
Debit   <u>3,710</u> (True loss)

# Sales on Installment

Even though this might not be a very popular type of practice, some companies use the method of installment sales as part of their daily business. With installment sales, a company makes a trade and decides to collect the payment over a period. That means if a company makes a sale of $900,000 on January 1, 2013, with a **sales on installment contract**, it can elect to collect the payments over any given period, and the amount outstanding equates to accounts receivable.

Note that, for transactions of this nature, the revenue from the sale as it is received is recognized along with the related gross profit. (Ignoring interest charges for this example).

### Illustration L

Let's assume a very simple transaction where JOAH Trading sold $900,000 of inventory with a cost of sales $540,000 to a customer on January 1, 2013, on a sales-on-installment contract. The agreement signed is for the customer to deposit $300,000 and the remaining amount of three equal installments with the first payment also due at signing.

Each installment will be $200,000 (900,000-300,000)/3
Amount due at signing is $500,000 (deposit of $300,000 plus first installment of $200,000)
Gross profit is $360,000 (900,000-540,000)
Gross profit rate 40% (360,000/900,000)

The journal entries for the sale would be as follow:

| Date | Account titles and explanation | Debit | Credit |
|---|---|---|---|
| 01/01/2013 | Installment accounts receivable | 900,000 | |
| | Inventory | | 540,000 |
| | Deferred G/P sales on installment | | 360,000 |
| | *To record deferred g/p sales on installment.* | | |
| 01/01/2013 | Cash | 500,000 | |
| | Installment accounts receivable | | 500,000 |
| | *To record cash receipt 1$^{st}$ installment plus deposit.* | | |
| | Deferred G/P sales on installment | 200,000 | |
| | Realized G/P sales on installment | | 200,000 |
| | *To record realized g/p on sales on installment (500,000\*0.4).* | | |
| 01/01/2014 | Cash | 200,000 | |
| | Installment accounts receivable | | 200,000 |
| | *To record cash receipt 2$^{nd}$ installment.* | | |
| 01/01/2014 | Deferred G/P sales on installment | 80,000 | |
| | Realized G/P sales on installment | | 80,000 |
| | *To record realized g/p sales on installment (200,000\*0.4).* | | |
| 01/01/2015 | Cash | 200,000 | |
| | Installment accounts receivable | | 200,000 |
| | *To record cash receipt 3$^{rd}$ installment.* | | |
| 01/01/2015 | Deferred G/P sales on installment | 80,000 | |
| | Realized G/P sales on installment | | 80,000 |
| | *To record realized g/p sales on installment (200,000\*0.4).* | | |

Please be aware that the total credit balance in the account Deferred Gross Profit sales on installment is now transferred to **Realized Gross Profit sales on installment** to keep the books balanced.

# Retainage

This type of receivable is familiar with companies that handle contractual work projects. A company can have a contract to perform some form of work for a client, and the client retained or withheld a portion of the contractual cost until there is assurance of satisfactory completion of the project. This type of receivable is called a *retainage*.

## Illustration L1

How it works: Let us assume that Premier Business Services was contracted to perform $200,000 worth of accounting consultancy for client Z. After paying periodic advances to Premier, the client in their interest would withhold at least 5% of the value of the contract $200,000 which is $10,000. Client Z would want to make sure that the completion of the entire project is in accordance with the terms and conditions of the contract before paying out the final amount of $10,000.

The journal entries would be as follow:

| Date | Account titles and explanation | Debit | Credit |
|---|---|---|---|
| 01/01/2015 | Cash | 100,000 | |
| | Service revenue | | 100,000 |
| | *To record cash collected as first deposit.* | | |

| Date | Account titles and explanation | Debit | Credit |
|---|---|---|---|
| 02/01/2015 | Cash | 50,000 | |
| | Service revenue | | 50,000 |
| | *To record cash collected as second deposit.* | | |

| Date | Account titles and explanation | Debit | Credit |
|---|---|---|---|
| 03/01/2015 | Cash | 40,000 | |
| | Service revenue | | 40,000 |
| | *To record cash collected as third deposit.* | | |

| Date | Account titles and explanation | Debit | Credit |
|---|---|---|---|
| 03/01/2015 | Accounts receivable | 10,000 | |
| | Service revenue | | 10,000 |
| | *To record retainage held by customer.* | | |

**Note that,** as soon as the client is fully satisfied that the completion of the work is in accordance with the contractual agreement; the remaining $10,000 is paid over to Premier Business Services. Cash account would be debited and accounts receivable credited.

# Loans Receivable

Within the Banking Sector, all loans disbursed whether long term or short term are considered receivables. It is the same description as in any other non-bank scenario.

## Illustration L11

If Premier Business Services granted Company Z a loan of $50,000, this money represents a receivable for Premier.

The journal entry would be:

| Date | Account titles and explanation | Debit | Credit |
|---|---|---|---|
| 01/01/2015 | Loans receivable | 50,000 | |
| | Cash | | 50,000 |
| | *To record loan granted to Company Z.* | | |

# Factoring Arrangement

As explained by the disposition of receivable section of this book, whether a company sells their receivable with or without recourse, the factoring company always withhold a portion of the proceeds to facilitate any adjustments such as sales discount or sales return. The net amount of the balance *"due from factor"* is receivable on the part of the selling company.

# Rebates

Sometimes a company purchases a particular item, and the selling company makes a promise to give a rebate or refund on the purchase price. This promised rebate is at most times part of the purchasing agreement.

## Illustration L111

If Premier Business Services purchased ten computers from Company Z for $48,000 and the selling company promised Premier a 2% rebate on the purchase price.

Premier would make the following journal entries:

| Date | Account title and explanation | Debit | Credit |
|---|---|---|---|
| 01/01/2015 | Computer equipment | 48,000 | |
| | Cash | | 48,000 |
| | *To record the purchase of 10 computers.* | | |

| Date | Account titles and explanation | Debit | Credit |
|---|---|---|---|
| 01/01/2015 | Rebate receivable | 960 | |
| | Computer equipment | | 960 |
| | *To record rebate receivable from computer purchase.* | | |

# Investment in Debt Securities

Whenever companies have excess cash on hand, they invest it in Commercial Papers, Certificate of Deposits, Treasury Bills, Bonds or Notes issued by other Companies, Banks or Government Agencies. Under these arrangements, the investing companies are expected to receive interest revenue and at a future maturity date the principal amount originally invested.

Therefore, since the companies who made these investments are to receive or recollect this money at some future date, if they have earned interest and not yet collected it then it would become interest receivable. Further to that, if the maturity date of the investments has passed, then the principal amount can now be classified as a receivable.

## Illustration L1V

A simple example would be Premier Business Services on December 31, 2012, decided to invest $120,000 in a Debenture Bond on par with an interest rate of 10% that matures in three years. Interest is payable on December 31 each year. Premier is expecting to collect the principal of $120,000 on December 31, 2015, along with any interest earned during the same period.

If on December 31, 2015, which is the maturity date of the bond, Premier has not collected a check representing the principal amount plus the interest for 2015, then the total amount would now be receivables on the books.

On December 31, 2015 (maturity date), the journal entry to record the interest earned during 2015 but not yet collected along with the principal is as follows:

| Date | Account titles and explanation | Debit | Credit |
|---|---|---|---|
| 12/31/2015 | Interest receivable | 12,000 | |
| | Debt investment receivable | 120,000 | |
| | Interest Revenue | | 12,000 |
| | Debt Investment | | 120,000 |

# Investment in Equity Securities

Another type of activity that generates some form of receivables is the investment in equity securities. Companies do make investments in stocks (preferred or common) of other companies in return for a dividend and this dividend once declared becomes a receivable to the investing company.

Please see the section under Dividends Receivable for the journal entry.

# Letter of Credit

Let us first try to gain an understanding of exactly what a Letter of Credit does. If a company is conducting business with a client whom they are uncertain about as it relates to their credibility of honoring a debt, the company requests a Letter of Credit from the client's bank in an effort that the bank is prepared to settle the debt on behalf of the client.

This type of arrangement is usually done by the company's bank and the client's bank to facilitate international trade, especially as it relates to import and export. It is easier for any company to accept a commitment for payment from a bank than from that of a client with whom they are experiencing some level of uncertainty.

Therefore, the creditworthiness of the bank issuing the letter of credit substitutes for that of the client and any receivable created in this transaction is honored by the client's bank.

The journal entry for this type of transaction is similar to that of a typical sale made on credit.

The following diagram shows you a typical flow of the transaction involving a letter of credit in an export/import scenario:

## Illustration LV

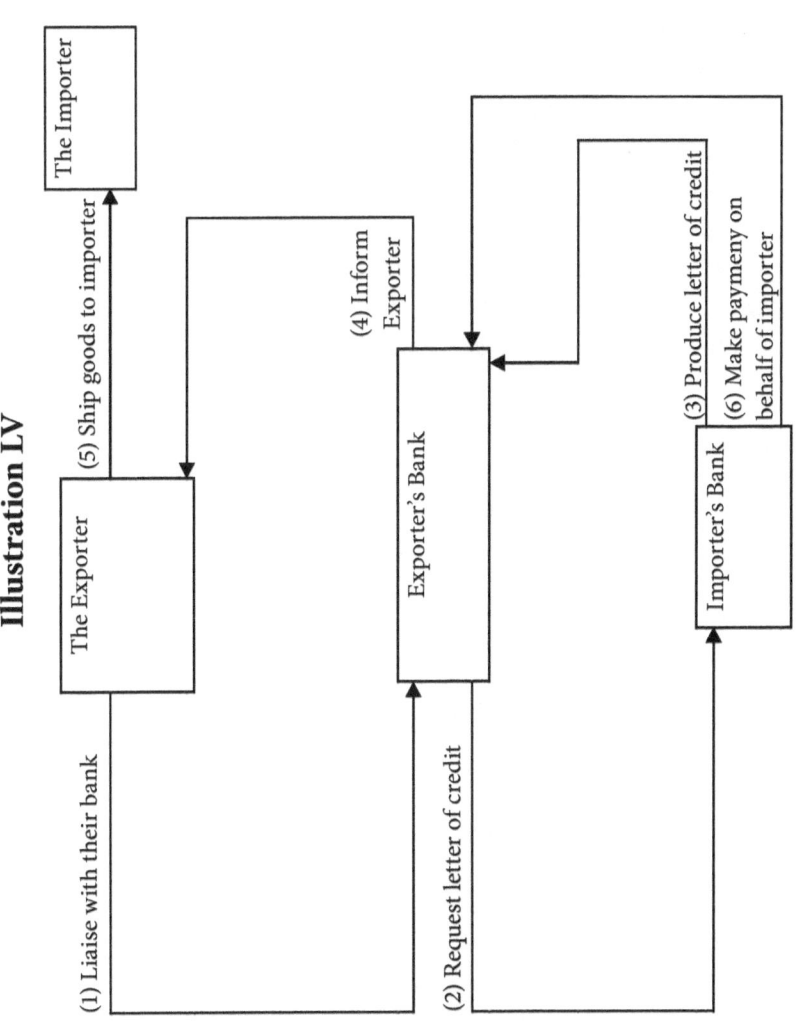

# Standby Commitment

Sometimes companies want some form of assurance or certainty that they can convert their receivables into cash and because of this, they put in place an arrangement called a Standby Commitment to Purchase. This commitment is an agreement between the company with the receivables and a Finance Company.

Once the company puts this arrangement in place, it allows them some flexibility of knowing that the Finance Company can readily purchase their receivables if the need arises.

# Mini cases

**Playing with the numbers**

As an Accounting professional, you may be confronted with an ethical issue that places you in a position to make a decision that affects your paycheck or to uphold proper accounting standards.

Since there are no hard rules against how management arrives at accounting estimates, just imagine you were asked to place an increase or a decrease in bad debt expense so that it could provide the needed impact on a year's profit or loss.

Example: You are being asked to make the income statement of your employer's business looks good because they are interested in securing a loan from a major commercial bank. The estimate of the bad debt expense for the year is one of the numbers you have been asked to manipulate so as to show a profit.

What is the possible response to your employer?

**Suggested answer**

Apart from the fact that your primary responsibility is keeping the books in a very efficient and accurate manner, it is also your job to guide your employer regarding how the numbers speak in accounting. While your employer is asking you to fix the numbers for this current period, because of their desire for a loan. You must be mindful of the fact that any smart Loans Manager at the Bank can ask for at least two to three previous periods of financial numbers. He or she would be conducting a careful analysis of those past periods along with the current fiscal year. Anything that looks strange would immediately send a signal for further investigation. Therefore, be careful. Don't try to manipulate the accounts to suit anyone. Be ethical and be a person of probity and rectitude.

## Credit Card vs. Store Cards

There has been an increase in the number of store cards being used by merchants to appeal to their customers, but before any store starts issuing a store card, there are some things they must take into consideration before they make that final decision.

As the Accounting professional, you are called upon to make a contribution regarding how this decision could affect the profitability of the company.

**Your advice**

Firstly, for any credit sales, there must be a measure of the benefit compared with the cost. Whether it is the use of store cards or third party credit cards, the main advantage is that you are attracting customers who like the idea of using cards.

With the use of credit cards, the seller does not incur a cost for assessing customers based on their credit. Also, the seller does not carry a credit risk of the customers not paying, and they also would receive their cash faster which is positive for cash flow.

On the other hand, having your store card would eliminate the credit card fees and even allows you the possibility of collecting revenue from interest and penalty charges to customers.

After careful analysis, you should be able to make a wise decision.

**Monitoring your accounts receivable turnover**

Like any other ratio, the accounts receivable turnover ratio is vital. There is a need to pay careful attention to how low or high this rate is. One thing for certain, if it is too low compared to the other businesses within the industry which you operate, this is a serious cause for concern.

Let us examine a case where you have done an analysis of your credit customers regarding how fast you are collecting the receivables outstanding.

Imagine you are the accountant for a struggling wholesale trading business and after an in-depth analysis you have discovered that a significant part of the reason your company is not profitable is that the rate at which your company is collecting its receivable is too low.

**Your recommendation**

A low accounts receivable turnover is a cause for concern, especially when compared to other companies in the same type of business. One of the first things to do is a review of the credit policy the company has in place.

Give greater attention to the customers whom credit has been extended either by rewarding the ones who can pay early with good sales discount or by retaining a credit card for the ones with not so good credit ratings. There might be a need to seek the assistance of a debt collector for the ones with long outstanding balances.

**Bad debt expense and making allowance for doubtful accounts.**

Bad debt expense and making allowance for doubtful accounts at times can be very confusing to understand by the persons who are non-accountants. There are times when the bad debt expense is more than the balance in the allowance for doubtful accounts for a given period.

Imagine being asked to explain to a team of people the rationale why something like this could happen.

In determining the ending credit balance in the allowance for doubtful accounts, always apply a percentage calculation to the balance in the accounts receivable or of the credit sales. The amount charged to bad debt expense for the period, is based on a calculation involving the ending (new) balance and the beginning (previous) balance.

If the beginning (previous) balance is a credit balance, then a simple subtraction of the two numbers (two credit balances) will give you the bad debt expense for the year.

Alternatively, if the beginning credit balance was adjusted to a debit balance throughout the year, it means that the previous estimate (beginning balance) for the allowance for doubtful accounts was under estimated because the total uncollectible written off exceeds that amount. Therefore, the bad debt expense for this scenario would be equal to the ending (new) balance in the allowance for doubtful accounts plus the excess (debit balance in the allowance for doubtful accounts) written off.

# Glossary

### These terminologies are accounting related

**Account** - A unit of record for a financial transaction.

**Account balance** - The difference between the amount on the debit side and the credit side of an account.

**Accounts receivable** - Any monetary value that a company has the right to receive from its vendors.

**Accounts receivable turnover** - The rate at which collection of accounts receivable occurs.

**Accrual** - This is the recognition of expenses when *incurred* even though no payment of cash has been made yet, and recognition of income when *earned* even though no cash has been collected yet.

**Analyzing a transaction** – The process of determining whether a business transaction affects asset, liability or equity.

**Asset** - Any value of ownership that has future economic benefit.

**Bad debt** - A debt the company deemed uncollectible.

**Balance Sheet** - A statement that shows a company's financial balances regarding assets, liabilities and equity at a *certain point* in time.

**Cash Discount** - This is the reduction in the price charged by the seller or service provider to encourage the buyer to pay earlier than the due date of the invoice.

**Credit** - The posting of an entry on the right-hand side of an account in a double entry accounting system.

**Current Asset** - This is cash or any other asset which is expected to be converted into cash, sold or consumed within a business operating cycle or one year, whichever is less.

**Customer** - This is the person who purchases your goods or services.

**Debit** - The posting of an entry on the left-hand side of an account in a double entry accounting system.

**Deferral** - This is money prepaid for an expense before it incurs or money collected as revenue before earned: Example pre-paid rent or unearned revenue.

**Doubtful account** - An account created to take care of a doubtful debt.

**Doubtful debt** - A debt that is uncertain to collect. An estimated calculation is used to determine this debt.

**Equity** - This is the owner's interest in an asset.

**Expenses** - This is any cost incurred to generate revenue.

**Factoring** - The selling of accounts receivables.

**Fair Value** - The unbiased price that would be received to sell an asset or paid to transfer a liability between buyers and sellers on a particular date.

**Foreign currency** - Any money that is not of your currency (Another country's money).

**Generally Accepted Accounting Principle (GAAP)** - This is the set of governing guidelines for accounting practitioners within the United States of America.

**Income Statement** - A statement that shows a company's financial performance based on profit or loss during a particular period. It shows you total revenues minus total expenses.

**Income tax** - A percentage of income earned that is paid to a Government agency.

**Journal** - The first book of entry that all accounting transactions are recorded before posting to the Ledger.

**Lease** - This is a written agreement allowing someone to use your property for a given period.

**Ledger** - The book of entry for accounting transactions after recording in the journal.

**Lessee** - This is the person who uses the property under the lease agreement.

**Lessor** - This is the person who authorizes the lessee to use the property under the lease agreement.

**Letter of credit** - This is, for example, a letter from a bank guaranteeing payment to a third party on behalf of its client.

**Operating Cycle** - This is the average time a business takes to acquire material or inventories and then convert it to cash.

**Periodic inventory system** - This facilitates the update of the merchandise inventory balance on a periodic basis by way of a physical count.

**Perpetual inventory system** - This facilitates the update of merchandise inventory balance on an ongoing basis by way of an accounting software.

**Post** – An accounting entry made in the ledger.

**Promissory note** - This is a written agreement to settle a debt.

**Recognizing a transaction** – The process of analyzing and recording a business transaction in the journal.

**Record** – An accounting entry made in the journal.

**Recourse (with)** - This is the opportunity to get help if someone is unable to satisfy an obligation of debt.

**Recourse (without)** - This is the *lack* of opportunity to get help if someone is unable to satisfy an obligation of debt.

**Remit** - To send or transmit money from one place to another.

**Retainage receivable** - This is a percentage of the total cost to complete a project that is withheld by a client until satisfactory completion is confirmed.

**Revenue earned** - This is the money collected or to be collected for goods sold or services performed.

**Security** - This is a *primary interest* in mostly stocks, bonds or notes evidenced by some form of documents.

**Service** - The performance of economic activity: For example, an Accountant preparing your tax return.

**To post** - To make an entry or note of an accounting transaction in a Ledger.

**To record** - To make an entry or note of an accounting transaction in a Journal.

**Trade Discount** - This is a reduction in the price charged by the seller of goods or provider of services based on bulk purchasing by the buyer.

**Trial balance** - This is a listing of all account balances from the ledger.

# Index

## A

Accounting cycle  3
Accounts Receivable  15, 19, 23, 24, 29, 30, 32, 33, 34, 40, 41, 42, 46, 47, 48, 49, 50, 53, 57, 64, 65, 70, 100, 108, 124
Accounts receivable ratio  108
Accounts receivable reconciliation  17
Accounts Receivable System  15, 19
Accounts Receivable Turnover  108
accrual system  11
Allowance Method  51
Amortization schedule  88, 90, 93, 95
average collection period  109

## B

Bad debt  47, 52, 54, 56, 60, 61, 63, 144, 145
Bad Debt  48, 49, 52
Bad Debt Recovered  49
Balance Sheet  7, 10, 13, 53, 55, 76, 78, 99, 145
Balance sheet method  51

## C

Cash discount  27
cash flow  15, 100, 106, 142
Certificate of deposits  135
Collection agency  17
Commercial papers  135
conservatism  99, 102
Conversion of accounts receivable  77
credit  1, 4, 9, 14, 15, 16, 17, 19, 20, 22, 25, 31, 32, 33, 34, 36, 37, 38, 39, 44, 47, 51, 55, 58, 59, 61, 63, 67, 68, 69, 73, 100, 108, 121, 126, 129, 139, 142, 143, 144, 145, 148
Credit card payment  16
credit check  15
credit policy  15, 143
current assets  12, 15, 76, 78

## D

Debenture bond  135
debits  1, 4
Deferred gross profit  129
Destination Point  6
Direct financing  112
Direct Write-Off  48, 64
direct write-off method  47, 50, 51, 58
Discount  27, 31, 32, 33, 42, 46, 88, 89, 90, 91, 95, 96, 146, 149
Discount on notes receivable  88, 89, 90, 91, 95, 96
dividend  120
doubtful account  52, 54, 55, 56, 57, 58, 59, 60, 61, 64, 66, 144

## E

Effective interest method  90, 93, 95
effective interest rate  86

effective method 89, 90
Employee training 17
end of period adjustment 79
Equity 7, 9, 10, 146
Equity securities 137
Expenses 5, 8, 9, 146

## F

face value 72, 74, 81, 82, 84, 86, 87, 92, 95
Factoring 14, 100, 101, 103, 146
fair value 97, 98
Foreign Currency 69

## G

General Ledger 23, 24, 49, 52, 57, 64, 65
goods 6, 15, 17, 20, 32, 39, 40, 41, 42, 43, 45, 47, 68, 81, 82, 116, 146, 149
Gross Method 29
Gross method - Periodic 33
Gross method - Perpetual 32

## H

Historical cost 97
honoring of the note 75, 76, 77, 78

## I

implicit rate 94
Income Statement 8, 9, 76, 78, 99, 147
Income statement approach 55
Income Tax Receivable 123
installment sales 128
Insurance Claims 126
interest bearing 72, 81, 82, 95
Interest Bearing Note 86, 94

Interest receivable 80, 114, 115, 117, 118, 119
invoice 1, 16, 20, 21, 27, 28, 29, 30, 32, 33, 34, 39, 42, 45, 69, 70, 105, 146

## J

journal v, 1, 4, 17, 20, 22, 31, 40, 41, 42, 43, 45, 67, 70, 75, 84, 89, 90, 91, 94, 96, 102, 103, 104, 105, 106, 110, 112, 116, 119, 120, 121, 122, 123, 125, 126, 129, 130, 147

## L

Lease Receivable 111
lessee 111, 112, 147
lessor 111, 112, 116
Letter of credit 138
Liabilities 7, 10
Lock Box 26
Long-term liabilities 10
Long-Term Notes 98

## M

Market interest rate 82, 86
market (yield) rate 82
Matching Principle 50, 51
maturity date 75, 76, 78, 79, 82, 95
Merchandise 31, 32, 41, 42, 45

## N

Net method 30
Net Method 29
Normal Balances of Accounts 9
note receivable at a discount 86
note receivable issued at a premium 91

## O

Open door policy 18
Operating lease 111

## P

Percent of total receivables 51
Periodic Audit 18
periodic inventory system 31
perpetual inventory system 31
Premium on notes receivable 92, 93, 94
present value 82, 83, 84, 87, 91, 92, 94, 116
principal amount 75, 76, 78, 83, 85, 87, 91, 92, 114, 117
Prior debit balance 61
promissory note 72, 74
Promissory Note 72

## R

Realized gross profit 129
rebate 134
Rebate 134
Receivables 11, 13, 15, 102, 104
recourse liability 101, 102
remit 26, 67, 102
rent receivable 110, 111
retainage 130, 131
Retainage 14, 130, 149
Return of the merchandise 39, 42
Revenue 4, 5, 9, 23, 29, 30, 31, 32, 33, 70, 75, 76, 78, 79, 80, 81, 149

## S

sale on installment contract 128
Sales Allowances 39
Sales discount 27, 29, 30
sales receipt 67
Sales Returns 39
Sales-type lease 116
security 14, 100, 106
services 15, 17, 22, 47, 73, 75, 79, 81, 146
Shipping Point 6
Short-Term Notes 98
Short-term notes receivable 74
Standby Commitment to Purchase 140
stated interest rate 72, 82, 83, 86, 87, 91
Store card 16
Straight line method 88

## T

Term Notes Receivable 81
The dishonoring of a note 78
Trade discount 27
Treasury bills 135

## V

Valuation of Notes 97

## W

without recourse 101, 104
with recourse 101

## Y

yield rate 86

## Z

zero interest 81, 94, 95
Zero-interest-bearing note 86

www.ingramcontent.com/pod-product-compliance
Lightning Source LLC
Chambersburg PA
CBHW032021170526
45157CB00002B/797